Warsas

and the

Hamble River

A History and Guide

Bryan Woodford.

Bryan Woodford

The west side of the Clock Tower, Warsash

Of all the slumberous rivers, none is more Lethean than the Hamble.

The morning mist dwells there, and the resonant call for the ferry

recalls the rhythm in which the Grecian poet Anacreon describes

the swan floating down the Little Meander.

But it is the beauty of the noon tide repose,

and not the beauty sleep of innocence.

The Hampshire Independent Newspaper, 1902

WARSASH PUBLISHING

Warsash Publishing
6 Dibles Road
Warsash
Southampton SO31 9HZ

ISBN (10 digit) 0948646845
ISBN (13 digit) 9780948646843

British Library cataloguing in Publication Data.
A catalogue record for this book is available from the British Library.

Produced by Solent Design Studio Limited, Hampshire, England.

Printed in Great Britain.

Front cover picture: An aerial view of Warsash and the Hamble River, with the Harbour Master's Tower and Stone Pier Boatyard near the centre of the image. Picture courtesy of Southern Daily Echo.
Back cover pictures: The ceramic tiles on the exterior wall of the Rising Sun Hotel; the cottages in Shore Road.

Dedication

This book is dedicated to my grandchildren, Steve, Katherine and Lewis Woodford, knowing that they appreciate, and enjoy living in, such a pleasant area, where their ancestors have resided for at least 150 years.

I would like to show my appreciation to Steve, who tirelessly taught me how to use a computer!

I also would like to thank my wife Margaret for her patience, tolerance and help during the past three years, whilst I have sat at a computer, or simply vanished to Hook with Warsash researching material relating to this book.

Contents

The Author's Family Biography

The author Bryan Woodford was born in Warsash in 1933, and attended school throughout the Second World War. He served an apprenticeship as a yacht and boat builder with A H Moody and Son at Swanwick, and on completion enlisted in the Royal Navy, serving twenty-three years in the Shipwright branch. After leaving the Royal Navy he became employed by the Shipbuilding Industry Training Board teaching apprentices the skills of traditional and modern yacht and boat-building.

His grandfather Henry Woodford, a boat builder and carpenter, resided and worked in Hamble, where Bryan's father Edward, known as Ted, was born in 1901. The family moved to Warsash in 1908, where Ted, also a carpenter, lived to be 92 years of age. Ted's brother Douglas also became a boat builder and shipwright.

Bryan's maternal great-grandfather George Light was a master mariner, residing in Hamble in 1861.

The entrepreneur James Lock, a close relative, played a considerable part in the growth of the village, including the trade in crabs and lobsters.

Margaret, the author's wife, is also from a local family with her great-grandfather, Walter Emery, a shepherd, living in the gamekeeper's cottage on the Hornby Estate in Hook circa 1880. Grandfather James Crockford became a prominent strawberry grower circa 1900, and her father served in the engineering branch of the Royal Navy. Margaret has been employed by the Warsash School of Navigation, a shipping agent, A H Moody and Son, Interyacht, the yacht broking company, and finally for twenty years in the library at the Warsash Maritime Academy.

Bryan is a committee member of the Warsash Local History Society, and vice-chairman of the Royal Naval Shipwrights and Artisans Association.

Memories have been passed down by his ancestors, from his wife and friends, and his own recollections, experiences and research.

Information, paintings, maps and photos have also been gathered from many diverse sources, including private persons, record offices, private collections, libraries, portrait galleries, a stately home, national newspapers, books and museums in Britain, the USA and Australia.

Introduction

The history of the two villages forming the parish of Hook with Warsash is interwoven with the maritime activities of the lower reaches of the Hamble River, which flows into Southampton Water and The Solent. The parish also includes the districts of Fleet End, Chilling and part of Brownwich.

The account covers the wooden warship building days from 1807 to 1813, the fishing boats during the crab and lobster era, industries, village inns and strawberry cultivation.

Many wealthy and influential persons resided in, or visited, the grand mansions, the large estates and the airfield. Yachting and boat-building were also principal activities during the 20th century with the Warsash Maritime Academy providing training for Merchant Navy deck and engineering personnel.

The author has conducted several guided walks in the village, with members of the Warsash Local History Society, describing places and people en route. These have proved successful, therefore he has written this book in a similar manner.

A map of the parish is included, which together with the details in the book may prove to be a guide to readers wishing to walk along our pleasant shoreline and through the village roads.

The main roads in the parish, with the smaller roads off them, each form a chapter, with over two hundred photographs, illustrations and maps, portraying properties, persons, yachts, vehicles and events. The Coastal Footpath is written in a similar way.

Four of the roads radiate from the Clock Tower at the centre of the village.

The Naval and Commando operations and civilian activities during the Second World War are described in a separate chapter.

The period covered is approximately two hundred years, from 1770 until 1970, although there are instances of earlier dates, and occasionally the details are up to the 21st century.

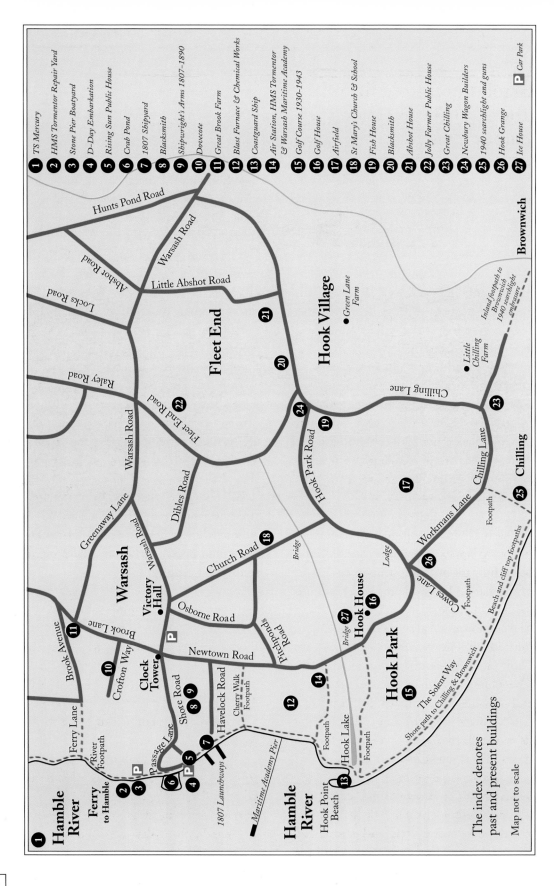

1. TS Mercury
2. HMS Tormentor Repair Yard
3. Stone Pier Boatyard
4. D-Day Embarkation
5. Rising Sun Public House
6. Crab Pond
7. 1807 Shipyard
8. Blacksmith
9. Shipwright's Arms 1807–1890
10. Dovecote
11. Great Brook Farm
12. Blast Furnace & Chemical Works
13. Coastguard Ship
14. Air Station, HMS Tormentor & Warsash Maritime Academy
15. Golf Course 1930–1943
16. Golf House
17. Airfield
18. St Mary's Church & School
19. Fish House
20. Blacksmith
21. Abshot House
22. Jolly Farmer Public House
23. Great Chilling
24. Newbury Wagon Builders
25. 1940 searchlight and guns
26. Hook Grange
27. Ice House

P Car Park

Hamble River
Ferry to Hamble

Hunts Pond Road

Warsash Road

Abshot Road

Locks Road

Raley Road

Little Abshot Road

Fleet End

Warsash Road

Greenaway Lane

Fleet End Road

Dibles Road

Warsash

Victory Hall

Brook Lane

Brook Avenue

Ferry Lane

River Footpath

Crofton Way

Clock Tower

Shore Road

Passage Lane

Maritime Academy Pier

1807 Launchways

Havelock Road

Cherry Walk Footpath

Newtown Road

Osborne Road

Pitchponds Road

Church Road

Bridge

Hook Village

Green Lane Farm

Chilling Lane

Little Chilling Farm

Hook Park Road

Hook House

Lodge

Cowes Lane

Bridge

Hook Park

Hook Lake

Footpath

Footpath

Workmans Lane

Chilling Lane

Chilling

Footpath

Beach and cliff top footpaths

The Solent Way

Shore path to Chilling & Brownwich

Hamble River

Hook Point Beach

Brownwich

Inland footpath to Brownwich to 1940 searchlight emplacure

The index denotes past and present buildings

Map not to scale

Brook Lane, from the Clock Tower to the junction with Barnes Lane

Warsash House, formerly situated between Shore Road and Crofton Way

Warsash House, a large mansion with an imposing appearance, was situated in a beautiful park in Hampshire in the South of England. Its gardens, which sloped to the Hamble River, also overlooked Southampton Water. This residence, located to the south of the present Crofton Way, was demolished in 1937. The white Edwardian gatekeeper's Lodge still remains 130 metres north of the Clock Tower in Brook Lane, which takes its name from a small stream, although much of it is now hidden in pipes.

A house is mentioned here in 1743 owned by John Brown which came into his possession on the death of his grandfather John Brown, and was named Passage House. The house was not of the grand style that it would eventually become during the next one hundred and ninety years.

George Newman became the owner in 1753, with Betty Purkis inheriting the estate in 1773.

In 1797 Captain Edward Foote RN was appointed to command HMS Seahorse, a frigate of 38 guns, and by 1800 he had purchased Passage House, also buying several other properties to add to the estate.

In 1810 the Honourable Cochrane Johnson, who had married a French widow from Martinique, became the next owner, but it was apparently not to their liking and it was sold one year later.

The Lodge in Brook Lane, the home of the gatekeeper, at the entrance to Warsash House

During 1811 the house became the residence of Thomas Lord Cochrane, the 10th Earl of Dundonald. He was one of the most daring captains of the Napoleonic wars, and nicknamed by the French *le loup de mer*, the Sea Wolf. He served in a wooden sailing frigate in 1805, similar to the ships built in Warsash. These small vessels were fast and manoeuvrable, and captured many enemy ships.

The British crews, particularly the captains, were paid large sums in prize money by the British government. The fictional career of Horatio Hornblower in the novels by C S Forester were partially modelled on the exploits of Lord Cochrane.

Lord Cochrane sold the property in 1817 to Captain Archibald Swinton, an employee of the East India Company, who greatly improved the house. Many titled persons visited Warsash including the second Duke of Wellington,

and the Marquess and Marchioness of Cholmondeley.

On the death of Archibald Swinton in 1843 the estate passed to his wife Louise, née Binfield, a clergyman's daughter.

It passed to her son Colonel Swinton in 1863, and he sold the property to Mr Edward Sartoris in 1868. Mrs Sartoris, née Adelaide Kemble, had been a famous opera singer before her marriage. Extensive improvements to the property gave it an imposing appearance in the Italianate style, with the mansion being renamed Warsash House. There were a fine hall, six reception rooms, seventeen bedrooms and dressing rooms and five bathrooms.

A carriageway lined with cedar trees, sweet chestnut, elm and scotch firs curved its way to the mansion through beautiful well-kept grounds, with an Italian flower garden and pillars, a fountain and a Florentine font.

A sunken rose garden made another feature near an artistic dovecote. This was built in a circular form, with uncoursed stone and a cote at the pinnacle, situated at the end of a topiary and pergola walk. The dovecote with its nesting places for three hundred birds can be seen near the entrance to Thornton Avenue.

Tennis courts were another feature in the gardens. Grapes, peaches and carnations were grown in large glass greenhouses in addition to other crops.

Mr Edward Sartoris became a Member of Parliament in 1886, his seat being in Carmarthenshire where he owned property named Llangennech Park. The artist Sir Frederic Leighton often visited Warsash House, where May Sartoris, Edward and Adelaide's daughter, sat in 1861 for her portrait, with local scenes that appear to be Sarisbury Church and Bursledon Windmill in the background. The painting is now displayed in the Kimbell Art Museum in Fort Worth, Texas.

May married Mr Gordon in 1871 and took residence in Warsash Lodge, now Warsash Court, in Havelock Road. King Edward VII also became an occasional

Mrs Adelaide Sartoris, a famous opera singer before her marriage, becoming a resident in Warsash House in 1868
© National Portrait Gallery, London

Portrait of Miss May Sartoris by Frederic Leighton, circa 1860. Oil on canvas, dimensions 152.1 x 90.2 cm.
© 2005 by Kimbell Art Museum, Fort Worth, Texas. Sarisbury Church and Bursledon Windmill in background

visitor to Warsash House while he was Prince of Wales.

Mr and Mrs Sartoris' younger son, Algernon, while travelling to America in 1872, met Miss Ellen Grant, the seventeen-year-old daughter of President Grant, formerly General Grant, with Algernon later proposing marriage. Ellen, generally called Nellie, was the President's only daughter, who was surrounded at home with affection and attention.

The President wrote to Mr Edward Sartoris in Warsash regarding his concern with Nellie marrying at a young age,

hoping that she would be at home for a few more years. Eventually the President gave his approval; Nellie and Algernon were married in the White House in Washington on 21st May 1874 to national and international acclaim. Returning to Warsash, they spent their honeymoon in Warsash Court. Later in 1877 President and Mrs Grant, during their tour of Europe, stayed in Warsash House.

Algernon and Nellie remained in Warsash and raised four children, with Algernon inheriting Warsash House in 1888, but dying in Capri in 1893. After

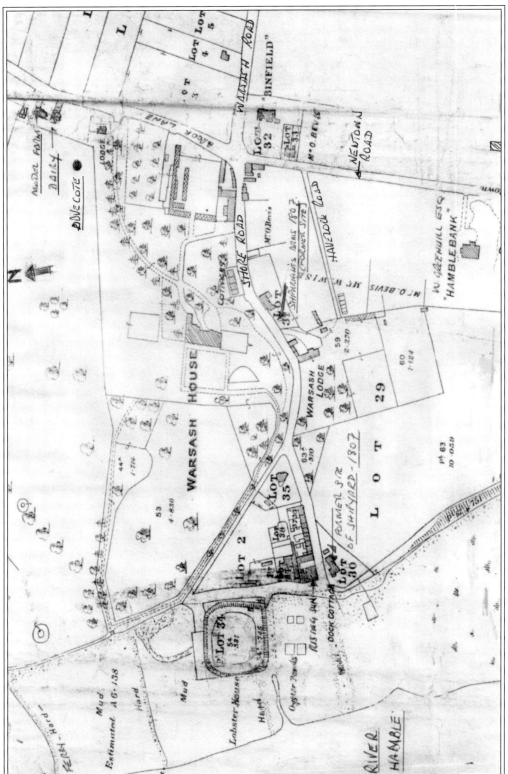

Map drawn in 1916, showing the lobster pond, Warsash House and Binfield (the Ferryman Public House)

nineteen years of marriage Nellie, who had generally spent the summer months with her parents, returned to live in America.

Ownership of Warsash House passed to Mr George Shenley, a wealthy American, in 1893.

During the next twenty-three years Mr Shenley, a keen yachtsman, made many improvements to the house and estate, building a large number of cottages for estate workers, and several other substantial houses. All the buildings were designed with character and have stood the test of time over one hundred years.

His *pièce de résistance* was the Clock Tower, proving very expensive to design and build. He had a flair for style and elegance that showed in his residence, his yachts and his many cars, some of which were painted bright yellow. His uniformed chauffeurs were smartly dressed, and several of his male staff wore their national Albanian costume, that caused much interest in Warsash.

Mr Shenley left the village in 1916 and the estate was sold by auction. Most of the houses and cottages were sold separately. The former common land in Brook Lane and Warsash Road was divided into approximately twenty-five plots and bought by individual persons, who were mainly strawberry growers. Bill Edmunds bought the corner plot at Warsash Corner, established a cycle repair shop, and later developed a car maintenance garage, with a supervisor and a mechanic. In 1932 radio repairs were also available after Bill had sent his nephew Bert to a Marconi training course.

Warsash man, Algernon Sartoris, with his wife Nellie, the president's daughter, in Washington in 1874
Courtesy of the Library of Congress, Washington DC LC-DIG-cwpbh 05127

The wedding of Nellie Grant, daughter of the President of the USA, to Algernon Sartoris, in the White House in Washington in May 1874. Courtesy of the Library of Congress, Washington DC LC-USZ62-94003

The President of the USA Ulysses Grant and his wife Julia visited Warsash House in 1877
Courtesy of the Library of Congress, Washington DC LC-USZ62-13018

Julia Grant, wife of the President of the USA
Courtesy of the Library of Congress, Washington DC LC-BH82-4559A

The dovecote at the far end of the topiary and pergola walk in the gardens of Warsash House in 1916

Sturdy timbers form the joists and roof structure of the dovecote (Author)

The dovecote, which can be seen near the entrance to Thornton Avenue, built circa 1810 (Author)

The interior of the stone dovecote, with nesting places for 300 pigeons or doves (Author)

Warsash House

The dining room

The library

Warsash House

The landing corridor

The Japanese bedroom

Warsash House

The drawing room

The staff in Warsash House

Warsash House

The hall of Warsash House

Another aspect of Warsash House, with the Italian garden

Mrs Shenley at the wheel of her husband's yacht

Warsash House Estate, properties and land in 1916

The estate consisted of over one hundred and twenty acres of land, a mansion, six superior residences, business premises, fifteen cottages, two farms, a dairy, coach houses and a garage, several large greenhouses, two smallholdings, a lobster pond and quay, and five acres of river bed and gravel hards.

All the estate properties were sold by auction in 1916 and are listed below.

Warsash House, with seventeen bedrooms, six reception rooms and fifty-five acres of grounds and park, formed the principal part of the estate. It was enclosed by Shore Road, the Hamble River, Brook Lane and Brook Avenue, with the exception of three acres of land belonging to Mr Toulson.

Warsash Lodge, now named Warsash Court, in Havelock Road, with seven bedrooms, three servants' bedrooms and fourteen acres of grounds.

The Haven, Shore Road.

Dock Cottage, now known as Shore House.

The head gardener's cottage in Warsash Road.

Stone Cottage in Shore Road.

Binfield, now The Ferryman Public House.

The Gate Lodge in Brook Lane.

Two cottages in Newtown Road.

Four cottages in upper Shore Road, now converted to two cottages.

Three cottages in lower Shore Road.

Brook House in Brook Lane.

Six cottages in Greenaway Lane.

Great Brook Farm in Brook Lane.

A dairy building in Brook Lane.

The Model Homestead farm buildings in Brook Lane.

The extensive Crab and Lobster House, tearooms and offices in Shore Road.

The crab and lobster pond and quays.

The boat house near the pond standing in a large plot of land.

The coal yard, office and shed in Shore Road.

Six acres of hards and mud on the shore, between low and high water marks.

The Clock Tower buildings, with staff accommodation, garages, coach houses, stores and stables.

Forty acres of land in Brook Lane, formerly part of Titchfield Common.

One acre of land near Swinton Hall.

Three acres in Brook Avenue.

A house with two acres of land in Hunts Pond Road in Titchfield Common was also included.

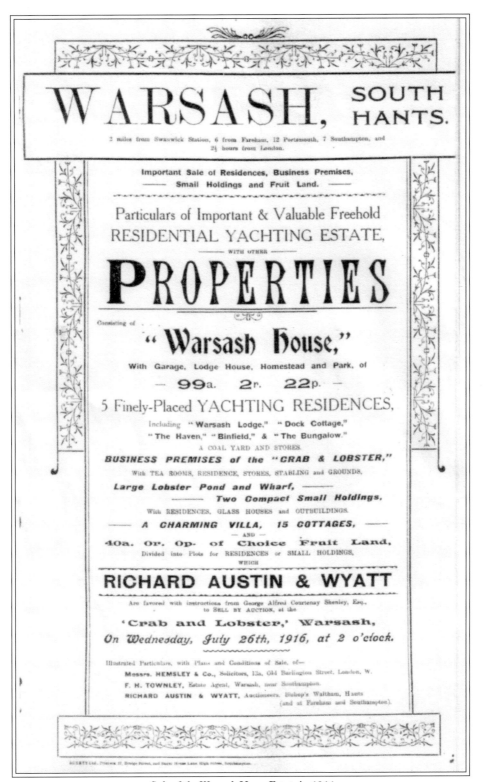

Sale of the Warsash House Estate in 1916

Montague Grahame-White purchased Warsash House in 1917

The next owner of Warsash House in 1917 was Lt Cdr Montague Grahame-White RNVR, who was serving in the Royal Naval Air Service during the First World War. He had been born in Bursledon Towers, now the site of the Tesco supermarket. Earlier, in 1877, he had shown enthusiasm as a car mechanic, also driving a Wolseley car in the 1900 Paris to Lyon road race, and became a founder member of the RAC.

During the First World War the European governments commandeered numerous large steam yachts, with all the vessels receiving extensive alterations to suit wartime needs. After the war the owners received government payments for reinstatement, but after seeing the poor condition of their ships many owners were inclined to keep the money and sell the vessels. The business acumen of Lt Cdr Grahame-White lay in buying these vessels at very favourable prices, contracting out the extensive repair and renovation work to a shipyard,

and finally selling the completed yachts at a profit. He also had the flair of improving the appearance of the yachts, in most cases replacing the old stovepipe-shaped funnel with one that was oval in appearance, which in turn increased the sales potential. Most of these yachts had schooner bows with bowsprits, and figureheads of two metres or more in length that were missing or damaged and had to be renewed.

A considerable amount of repair work and engine installation to launches and boats belonging to the various yachts refitting at Cowes or Southampton was

Montague Grahame-White's sister, Mrs James Gagé

The steam yacht Alacrity, owned by Montague Grahame-White,
which had her own moorings laid in the Hamble River

completed at Warsash in the workshops that Lt Cdr Grahame-White had built on the quay.

There were in total twenty-five steam yachts reconditioned between 1919 and 1929, varying in size from 58 to 1,800 tons, with many of them moored in the Hamble River opposite the Rising Sun before or after renovation, the largest being the twin screw Alacrity, 93 metres in length overall, with special moorings laid for her at a cost of £750 in 1925. When under full complement of crew she carried sixty officers and men. She was elegantly fitted out, with luxurious cabins, a grand curving staircase with balustrades, and staterooms, appearing more in keeping with a grand house ashore than a ship. A Russian Royal font, decorated with a figurine and other elaborate embellishments, stood in the main passage.

Another vessel that moored at Warsash for several years, also owned by Lt Cdr Grahame-White, was the 26-metre twin-screw motor yacht Astrid. She was used for transporting men and stores between Warsash, Cowes and Southampton in connection with the yacht renovation business in these ports. Grahame-White in 1919 also owned a seven-metre Saunders hydroplane that often went from Warsash to Cowes with a speed of 37 knots.

Claude Grahame-White, an early aviator, brother of Montague, often visited Warsash. He had been a pupil of Bleriot in France and opened an aviation works at Hendon in 1909.

Lt Cdr Grahame-White and his wife entertained many celebrities including the singers Dame Clara Butt and her husband Kennerley Rumfold. She became famous for singing Elgar's Land of Hope and Glory, written in 1911, which became very successful during the First World War, when patriotic music and songs were very popular. On one occasion after the First World War she performed at the

The main staircase of the steam yacht Alacrity

The main bedroom cabin of the steam yacht Alacrity

Montague Grahame-White's motor yacht Astrid circa 1927

Victory Hall in Warsash. Dame Clara had a very powerful voice, and it is worthy of note that a CD with Dame Clara singing is available today in 2006. In 1929 the Prime Minister Ramsey Macdonald and his daughter Isobel spent a weekend on board the Grahame-White yacht Ianara at Cowes during the Sneider trophy aircraft races. A few days later Sir Thomas Lipton, owner of the Shamrock J Class yachts, and the Marchese and Marchesa Marconi of early communications fame were entertained on board this beautiful vessel, which often moored in the river at Warsash. Sir Thomas had owned a large steam yacht named Erin, which the Admiralty requisitioned during the war. The teak panelling in the yacht was removed from the vessel before naval service and given to Montague Grahame-White in 1919, and later fitted to the main corridor in Warsash House.

In 1929 Lt Cdr Grahame-White sold Warsash House to Lord Stalbridge, who became the final owner to occupy the property. He was a keen yachtsman, owning a three-masted schooner, the Cetonia, which moored adjacent to the crab and lobster quay. In 1934 the house and gardens were sold to a property development company, who in 1937 demolished the house and built houses in Thornton Avenue and Crofton Way.

On the north side of the Thornton Avenue and Brook Lane junction stands the estate dairy, built in 1914, and considered very up to date at that time. It is built in stone with a thatched roof. The original building has been skilfully joined in recent years to a new dwelling and makes a very attractive home.

Next door resides Mr Roy Knight, in the former model homestead farm built by Mr Edward Sartoris. There were stables for eight horses and eight cows, a fowl house, pig sties and a granary on staddle stones. The farm was built in 1870, and was considered as being the best in farming, an example for others to follow. Roy's father, the village police officer, bought the property in 1938, intending to convert it into a dwelling with two garages when he retired from the Police Force. This was not to be until

The former Model Homestead Farm in Brook Lane in 1916

the end of the Second World War, in 1945, when building materials were extremely difficult to obtain. However, Mr Knight Snr and Roy, improvising with materials and skills, made the conversion a success. Roy and his wife Peggy were the village newsagents for thirty years, and on retirement made their home in this picturesque building and garden.

Roy was born in Warsash in 1928, and is very enthusiastic in studying the history of the village. In his possession is a large number of photos, books and paraphernalia collected by himself and the late Wyn Newbury. These have been on display several times in the Victory Hall, attracting on one occasion 800 visitors during a four-day exhibition.

In 1960 the famous aircraft pilot Peter Twiss OBE, DSC and Bar came to reside in Long Meadow, in Brook Lane, Warsash. His flying career had commenced in 1939 when he joined the Royal Navy wearing the square rig and bell-bottoms of a naval rating. He trained

in Tiger Moths and then flew Seafires from an aircraft carrier. Throughout the war he flew a very wide range of aircraft, leaving the Royal Navy in 1946 with the rank of Lt Commander. During the same year he became employed as a test pilot with Fairey Aviation, involved again with many aircraft, finally breaking the world high-speed record in a Fairey Delta aircraft at an average speed of 1,132 miles an hour in March 1956. The flight track for the test commenced at Boscombe Down and finished at Ford in Sussex, passing over Corhampton. The aircraft returned by the same route, with the time and speed measured between two points spaced fifteen miles apart. Later, in 1960, Peter became employed by Fairey Marine at Hamble, involved in the development and sales of a range of fast cruising motor yachts, capable of speeds of over 40 knots.

Nearing Greenaway Lane on the left is Brook House, also an earlier Warsash House estate property, with a carriage drive and sweep and servants' quarters.

Peter Twiss, OBE, DSC, aircraft world speed record holder at 1,132 mph, resided in Long Meadow in Brook Lane in 1960, seen here with Sir Billy Butlin passing the Rising Sun Hotel

It was originally built as accommodation for the estate bailiff.

Greenaway Lane, which turns off to the right, has a terrace of six interesting Edwardian cottages, built by Mr Shenley for the Warsash estate workers. Virtually all the land surrounding Greenaway Lane was cultivated with strawberries from 1916 to more recent times, owned by different people, each with three- to five-acre plots.

Opposite the entrance to Greenaway Lane is the impressive Great Brook Farm, built in the 16th century with a substantial farmhouse, two thatched barns, a granary on staddle stones and

Estate Cottages in Greenaway Lane

another thatched building. All appear in a well-maintained condition and were originally estate property.

Further on, approaching Brook Avenue, a house stands on the left forming part of Brook Farm as noted in the 1870 map. Mr Toulson was the farmer here in 1916, also owning land on the opposite side of the road and in Brook Avenue.

A footpath from Brook Avenue named Ferry Lane leads to the ferry which crosses to Hamble. It has been in use for centuries but is now reduced in width. It was described in the Fareham Definitive Map and Statement in 1995 as still being a highway.

The Warsash boundary is a short distance further, near the junction with Barnes Lane.

Great Brook Farm in 1916

Brook Lane in 1916 viewed from the Clock Tower crossroads

Index of successive owners of Passage House, renamed Warsash House

Date unknown Mr John Brown
1743   Mr John Brown, a brewer from Titchfield
1753   Mr George Newman
1773   Miss Betty Purkis
1796   Mr Peter Green, farmer
1800   Captain Edward Foote RN
1810   The Hon Cochrane Johnson
1811   Admiral Lord Thomas Cochrane RN
1817   Captain Archibald Swinton, East India Company
1843   Mrs Louise Swinton, wife of Archibald Swinton
1864   Mr W H Swinton, son of Archibald Swinton
1868   Mr Edward Sartoris, MP, of French descent
1888   Mr Algernon Sartoris, son of Edward
1893   Mr George Shenley, an American
1916   Mr Henry White
1917   Mr Montague Grahame-White, born at Bursledon Towers
1929   Lord Stalbridge, yacht and racehorse owner
1934   A property development company
1937   The house was demolished

The Coastal Footpath, from the Ferry Shelter to Hook Point, Chilling and Brownwich

In the year 1537, during the dissolution of the monasteries, donkeys grazed on the embankment of the Hamble River at a place known as Warish Asse Feld, later to be named Warsash.

Standing on the path at the ferry shelter, looking inland, an area covered with water and reeds can be seen close by, formerly water meadows until circa 1940. The river embankment became breached through erosion, causing these large fields where cows grazed to be flooded, creating intertidal mudlands. In circa 1980 repairs were made to the embankment, and it was again possible to walk to Sarisbury and Swanwick.

Large diameter pipes were laid through the embankment which allows seawater to pass in and out at each tide, creating a bird and wildlife habitat spread over many acres, with the original main bank of the river close by, bordered by woodland, where smugglers at one time were reputed to have hidden contraband in hollow oak trees.

In 1866 the Southampton and Netley Railway Company planned to build a railway line linking Portsmouth to Southampton. It contemplated continuing the existing line from Netley over the Hamble River by a swing bridge and through Warsash and Titchfield to Fareham, where it would join the London and South Western Railway.

A bill for this extension went before Parliament in 1866, but it was not built.

In 1882 the L&SWR decided to promote their own line from Netley to Fareham and plans were deposited in November.

The earlier plans for a swing bridge at Warsash were not repeated, and a high-level bridge upstream from the Bursledon Bridge Company's road bridge was proposed. This satisfied the Southampton Harbour Board, who at that time were responsible for the navigation on the Hamble River. The line opened in 1889 with intermediate stations at Bursledon and Swanwick.

The ferry to Hamble has been operating for many centuries, at least since 1493. Small boats were used, which were propelled with the use of oars, with horses which were known to be good swimmers attached with a rope, and towed astern as the boat was rowed across. The nearest bridge over the Hamble was at Botley until the wooden toll bridge between Bursledon and Swanwick was built in 1800.

During the 19th and 20th centuries shipwrights and other shipyard staff living on both sides of the river used the ferry to get to their work, constructing wooden warships, fishing vessels and small boats in Hamble and Warsash. Residents would use the ferry when travelling to Southampton, and walk the remaining four miles from Hamble. Occasionally they may have ridden in a horse brake until the advent of motor transport.

In 1905 Coopers the brewers, who also owned the Bugle Inn in Hamble, bought the ferry, and built the brick and cement rendered shelter on the Warsash shore in circa 1920. The ferry ran straight across the river taking the shortest distance to the gravel hard at Hamble, near the present sailing club. The rowing distance at low tide was therefore half of that at full tide, with bicycles being carried in the bow of the boat.

The introduction of outboard motors in circa 1939 made life easier for the ferryman and a faster journey for the passengers. During the 20th century many people worked in the large aircraft factories and boatyards in Hamble, ensuring passengers. As more people travelled in cars, and factories closed, passenger numbers dropped, although day-trippers did provide extra trade, with some taking children across for a pleasant walk around the village, an ice-cream and a chat with the ferryman.

A larger vessel constructed of steel, with an inboard engine, came into use in 1993. This was much safer when crossing a busy river, particularly at weekends. A new berth was made available solely for the ferry on the new jetty at Hamble. Although it is further to travel, the new arrangements make it easier for the passengers to embark and disembark.

Near the ferry shelter at Warsash a concrete anti-aircraft gun emplacement built in 1940 can be seen. The Bofors gun situated here was operated by the Royal Artillery, firing at German aircraft when they attacked the airfield and factories in Hamble or shipping in the river and Southampton Water during the Second World War.

A three-masted sailing barque named Illova, built in 1867, was purchased by the banker Mr C Hoare in 1885. She was renamed TS Mercury and moored off Binstead, in the Isle of Wight, and used as a training ship. During the year 1888

the ship sailed to the Mediterranean Sea with 130 boys and twenty experienced seamen.

The ship moved to a permanent mooring in the Hamble River in 1892, on the Hamble side, near the site of the present day Mercury Marina. The boys could be seen regularly in the ship's cutter, with twelve oarsmen all rowing in unison. In 1914 an ex-Royal Navy steam/sailing sloop, HMS Gannet, launched in 1878, fifty-eight metres in length, arrived in the Hamble. An ark-like structure was built over her decks, and she joined TS Mercury.

The TS Mercury (ex-Illova) was removed from service in 1916, with her successor HMS Gannet subsequently being renamed TS Mercury, and used as a dormitory ship. The lads slept in hammocks, which have a great advantage over bunks in a rough sea, as those who later joined the Royal Navy discovered. The training school closed in 1968, with the ship finally leaving the river in 1980.

A smaller vessel was owned by the director Mr Fry, and used as a seagoing tender to TS Mercury. She was the wooden-built auxiliary ketch Vishala, of 34 tons register, launched by J Scott of Montrose as the New Ranger in 1902.

On leaving TS Mercury a number of lads were able to obtain a one-year cadetship at the School of Navigation at Warsash before joining a Merchant Navy ship.

The Chatham Historic Dockyard Trust has now restored HMS Gannet to her original 1878 condition, and she is open to the public.

Between the Ferry and Stone Pier Boatyard can be seen four large concrete

The concrete blocks, situated between the Stone Pier Boatyard and the ferry, were used for mooring landing craft during the Second World War (Author)

blocks. They are close to the sea wall, although one has moved from its original position, and are 1.3 cubic metres in dimension. Each one has four chains embedded into it, which secured the bow ropes of Royal Navy landing craft moored there during the Second World War. The stern of each vessel was moored by using a kedge anchor, which is a stern anchor, dropped further out in the river, with the vessels lying at a right angle to the shore, and going aground at low tide.

Stone Pier Boatyard was originally a small private yard constructed on the lobster quay by Lt Cdr Montague Grahame-White in 1919, and later owned by Lord Stalbridge. It was greatly extended for the Royal Navy during the Second World War, and became the maintenance and repair yard

Mona Peckham and John Rowe, employees of the Tormentor Yacht Station, resting between races at the Hamble River Regatta

for HMS Tormentor, a combined services small craft base.

The yard was acquired after the war by Air Commodore Sir Adrian Chamier, KB, CMG, DSO, OBE, and named the Tormentor Yacht Station. Several types of small sailing craft were built, including Flying Fifteens, 505 dinghies and two Itchen Ferry fishing boats, all of wooden construction.

Two 12-metre boats were also built for the Custom Service. A 36-metre wooden harbour defence vessel was converted into an inshore minesweeper at the yard and delivered to the Royal Navy base HMS Diligence at Hythe, near Southampton, in 1958.

The boatyard was sold in 1960 to Woodnutt and Company, who also owned a boatyard in the Isle of Wight. Then the Stone Platt Group became the next owners for a short while. In 1963 the yard changed hands again and was purchased by A H Moody and Son of Swanwick. Two Fred Parker designed motor boats were built, followed by the Laurent Giles Salar 39 motor sailer project, and two six-metre in length motor launches designed by Graham Moody. In order to partially finance the construction of a new marina at Swanwick A H Moody and Son sold Stone Pier Yard in 1968.

Between the boatyard and The Rising Sun lays a large open area covered in concrete, which forms the laying-up yard for the Warsash Sailing Club. This area had originally formed a very large pond, where in 1870 James Lock kept crabs and lobsters, also using another pond on Hamble Point.

The Warsash crab pond was rebuilt in 1900, with the concrete outer walls forming a quay, with 65 metres of river

James Lock's pond in Hamble circa 1890

The Coastal Footpath

An aerial view of Warsash, dated 1925, with the crab and lobster pond and the Hamble River on the right hand side of the image.

frontage, where vessels of considerable tonnage could discharge their cargo. It was the only quay in the area, and with a crane that could lift up to five tons it provided a steady income for its owner.

Vessels from Warsash, with the traditional black hulls and brown sails, transported crustaceans from the West Country and Ireland which had been caught by the local fishermen.

Evidence that these boats went to Cornwall is shown in the census for vessels in harbour at Falmouth in Cornwall in 1881.

The Eagle is listed as a crabber, with Thomas Bevis, aged 49, a master fisherman, born in Warsash, William Baker, aged 54, fisherman born in Sarisbury, and Thomas B Bevis, aged 19, a fisherman, also born in Warsash.

Bill Godwin, crab boat skipper

James Lock weighing crabs in Warsash circa 1900

James Lock's first tearoom in Shore Road

The Crab and Lobster tearooms, dance hall and offices

Visitors to the Warsash pond were able to select their own crabs, crayfish or lobsters with satisfaction; this also gave much enjoyment to spectators. Day-trippers were coming to Warsash in large numbers from Fareham, Gosport and Portsmouth in horse-drawn brakes.

James Lock already ran a teashop on the waterfront, and quickly expanded his business. A large, attractive and prestigious new two-storey building was erected in 1903 on the site of the present Quay House apartments, adjacent to The Rising Sun, with offices, residential rooms and a large sail room that was also used for dances. The large first floor tearoom with excellent views over the river was well-patronised. There was also a detached

single-storey cloistered tea lounge, where patrons could also dine on the lawn.

James Lock bought his first crab boat on a shared basis, eventually acquiring eight more of his own. Most of these boats had been trading vessels, or, as with Cupid, a 12.5-metre pilot boat of 28 tons registration. Alterations were made to provide fish holds by fitting watertight bulkheads and boring a large number of 40mm diameter holes through the vessels' lower hull planking.

When at sea the motion of the vessel would allow seawater to circulate through the hold and keep the crustaceans alive until arrival at Warsash. They were then stored in the pond or in wooden boxes, with a hinged door on the top called a

Two of James Lock's crab and lobster carrying vessels

The Hamble River, with fishermen sitting on the crab storage carbs

carb. The carbs were approximately three metres in length, 1.5 metres wide, one metre high, and were moored in the river. When crabs were required to be removed the carbs were towed onto the hard at high tide, and as the tide receded their contents could be removed with ease. The crabs etc were eaten in James Lock's tearooms and other tearooms in Shore Road. Sales opportunities were made elsewhere including London, with the crustaceans being packed in wicker hampers and passing through Swanwick railway station. The requirement to transport crabs and lobsters from the West Country, for over a period of fifty years, declined in 1920. The hardworking boats were laid up in mud berths along the shore of the Hamble River, where many of their oak frames are still visible. Their names are still alive in village folklore: Bonnie Lass, Jemima, Cupid, Eagle, Gem, Harriet, Imogen, Jubilee and Stella.

The tea rooms, since the crab and lobster days, were used for many purposes, including a store for yacht equipment and a yacht broker's office. They were demolished circa 1980 and replaced with apartments.

The pond was used to store crabs and lobsters until 1959. About that time a restaurant named Eduardo's Cortijo opened opposite the pond in the single-storey tea room, continuing as a family run business until circa 1998. It was demolished in 2003 and replaced with three-storey dwellings painted cream.

It is recorded that the 'mud and hards' forming approximately six acres of foreshore, extending from the high watermark to the low water mark, and from the southern wall of the lobster pond northward to the Hamble Ferry hard, were owned by the Warsash House Estate and put up for auction in 1916.

Warsash gourmet

The next building is the attractive 'Ye Rising Sun with Strongs Romsey Ales' as the inscription set in coloured ceramic tiles on the outside wall informs us. The hostelry may well have been on the site of an earlier hotel. A photograph shows a former building with Sun Hotel written in large letters on the wall, with a swinging sign that reads 'The Rising Sun'. The present Rising Sun Hotel was built in 1906, with four bars. The Public Bar was strictly for men, with a smaller bar where women were welcome with husbands or men friends. The Bottle and Jug, as the name implies, where beer could be purchased to take away, overlooked the river, as did the Saloon Bar where furnishings were to a higher standard. All was overseen by the red-cheeked landlord Mr Dawkins, wearing a canary waistcoat, with a plump Dalmatian at his feet.

There is a tale regarding a group of people in 1920, who were drinking in The Rising Sun. They had come down from Warsash House, where they were staying as guests. A member of the party wagered a fiver that an army colonel in their party would not swim across the well-stocked crab and lobster pond. The

The former Sun Hotel

bet was accepted, the colonel took off his coat, shirt and shoes, plunged into the pond, swam to the opposite side without losing a toe, and within a few minutes was back in The Rising Sun. He bought a round of drinks with his winnings. Five pounds at that time was probably equal to two weeks' wages for a craftsman.

Through the pub windows can be seen the Public Hard, in earlier times the hub of the village, always a busy place, and it remains so: fishermen bringing the catch ashore which attracts buyers and others eager to see the fish; seagulls circling, children helping, dogs barking on their owners' return and smiling wives, for seafaring was a hazardous occupation. Ships loaded here with wheat, to be ground into flour at the tide mill at Ashlett Creek near Fawley. Trading ships under sail, and sprit sail barges, loaded with loam, timber, bricks, grain, china or coal, and many other items, in a manner that heavy goods vehicles carry goods today, would anchor in the river or moor at the quay, or lay on the beach for various reasons. It may have been to load or unload, to wait for the tide to turn, or that bad weather was imminent at sea, so the crews would come ashore. It was wiser to drink a beer in The Rising Sun than to face a strong gale in the setting sun.

During the Napoleonic Wars shipwrights travelled in the ferry from Warsash to Ashlett Creek, near Fawley, to work in the wooden warships being built at Lepe and Bucklers Hard.

The carriage of goods by sea continued until about 1920, when rail and motor vehicle transport superseded the requirement for coastal vessels.

The 20th century brought large steam and sailing yachts to the Hamble River, owned by wealthy local residents and crewed by Warsash men. To some extent this gave employment to the fishing boat crews who had been made redundant.

The yacht crew members wore blue jerseys with the name of the yacht written in white letters across the chest. These would be proudly worn ashore, particularly when the yacht had performed well in races. One of the larger vessels was the twin-funnelled steam yacht Triad, owned by Mr Shenley of Warsash House.

Another yacht in 1923 was the Dolphin, a square-rigged auxiliary brigantine of 176 tons, owned by Sir Warden Chilcott, who resided in The Salterns, a mansion in Newtown Road, now named Admirals House. The Dolphin often sailed to the Mediterranean Sea, where Sir Warden owned a castle in Corsica, and was often host to many distinguished guests.

Sir Austen Chamberlain, the British Secretary of State for Foreign Affairs, met the Italian dictator Mussolini on the yacht in 1926. On another occasion in 1935 Sir Austen and his wife Ivy, who resided in Warsash, were again on board, with Sir Warden's friend, Rosamond Contessa di Sant'Elia. The Contessa, who owned Springfields in Newtown Road, now named Kingswood House, was a very wealthy English woman, unhappily married to an Italian Count. The Contessa had joined the yacht Dolphin at Cannes, in the South of France, and wrote in her journal, "Chillie, as Sir Warden was called, met me on arrival. The crew were unchanged, James still the

*Sir Warden Chilcott KB, MP residing in The Salterns
The Times Literary Supplement, 20th October 1923*

*Ted Woodford, crew member of the brigantine
Dolphin in 1923, wearing the yacht's jersey with the
initials of the Royal Thames Yacht Club. He
previously served in Lord Birkenhead's yacht Mairee,
RYS, a converted French excise cutter which also
moored in the Hamble River*

*Sir Austen Chamberlain, British Secretary of State for
Foreign Affairs, 1924 to 1929, resided with his wife
Ivy in Red Tiles in Newtown Road, Warsash from
1935 to 1937. Photo The Times Literary Supplement,
20th October 1923*

*Rosamond Contessa di Sant'Elia circa 1935,
owner of Springfields in Newtown Road,
now know as Kingswood House*

steward, and the same Captain. The best cabin had been reserved for the Queen of Spain, who was to be a guest. Chillie was as if a cat on hot bricks, for the Queen had not yet arrived on the Riviera. He had taken a great fancy to this attractive Royal Lady, and became excited with the honour of receiving her. While waiting in Cannes for the Queen to arrive, we filled in time by visiting the casino for a little mild gambling, and whom should we find, but Princess Mafalda, the daughter of King Victor Emanuel of Italy, with the Riccios in tow, so we invited them to have tea on the Dolphin the following day. On boarding the yacht, the guests signed the visitors' book, and the women accepted a brooch, a green enamel dolphin, which Sir Warden presented to all his cruising guests.

"The days passed without any word from Spain, and as Ivy Chamberlain had planned the whole scheme, I could not but feel sorry for her.

"News arrived at last that the Queen and her party had changed their plans and were in Corsica, where they were to stay in Chillie's castle, with the Dolphin being required to sail quickly to Corsica. I was very interested in watching how Chillie got on with the Queen."

A page is quoted, taken from a Christmas card sent by Sir Warden to his friends and employees, appertaining to his yacht.

"The Indefatigable Training Ship Committee of Liverpool built the Brigantine Dolphin, first known as the James J Bibby of Liverpool, in 1902 for training boys for the Merchant Navy.

"A Sailing Master and sixty boys sailed her round the world, and some hundreds of lads became mariners in her prior to the outbreak of World War 1. In 1914 she was purchased by the Government and renamed Peggy of London. Her war service was spent in cruising about the North Sea as 'bait' for the German submarines. In this capacity she was instrumental in the destruction of many of these craft. Although on several occasions torpedoes attacked her, she always escaped without injury, a tribute either to the bad shooting of the German submarines or her own good luck, possibly both.

"After the war in 1922 her present owner, Lt Commander Sir Warden Chilcott MP, purchased this lucky ship and renamed her Dolphin. In 1923 she was redesigned, reconditioned and converted into an auxiliary yacht for her owner's use.

"During the season of 1925, between August and November, she made a cruise of 5,480 miles. Under her new arrangement and rig she proved herself a first-class sea boat with exceptional sailing qualities.

"The ship's motto is:
Though pleased to see the Dolphins play
I mind my compass and my way.

"While Dolphin was serving as an armed Q-ship during the war she opened fire when stopped by a U-boat, inflicting so much damage to the submarine that it surrendered to an armed trawler."

A converted French revenue cutter named Mairee also moored in the river, owned by Lord Birkenhead, the Lord Chancellor of Great Britain and friend of Sir Warden. In 1922, the Mairee sailed to Dieppe, continuing through the

French canals to the Mediterranean, and to Genoa. A reception was given for the King of Italy, the vessel then returning to England.

Sir Warden also owned two very fast powerboats that could carry a small number of passengers, the 16-metre Javelin, built in 1927 by Camper and Nicholson, similar to the craft used as tenders to J Class yachts, and the smaller Arrow.

He used Javelin to view the ships at the Naval Fleet Review at Spithead in 1935. The Contessa travelled with him, commenting on the glorious unforgettable sight, and a memory for a lifetime.

Returning the following evening to see the fleet lit up, she notes:

"We waited until darkness, and at precisely the same moment the whole fleet lit up, again at the same moment from each ship went up rockets making a bouquet of red, white and blue stars."

At that time British women who married a foreigner lost their British nationality. Therefore the Contessa Rosamond was considered to be an undesirable alien, and interned in Britain during the Second World War.

Javelin was restored by a new owner in 1989 and renamed Herring Gull. There was another similar craft named Suani on the river, owned by Mr H Ross and manned by Warsash man Harry Pannell. These vessels were of the Gelyce class; several were fitted with a larger engine and were capable of a speed of 21 knots.

Many fishermen found employment in yachts during the summer, with regular pay, better food and working conditions, some receiving a retainer and returning to their former occupation during the winter.

During the yacht racing season at Cowes vessels would arrive from all over the UK and abroad, with local fishermen being employed as pilots in yachts whose skippers were not familiar with The Solent.

In 1908 John Baker White, as a boy, lived in the bungalow at Chilling with his mother and stepfather, moving later to Flagstaff in Locks Heath and then to Warsash. Prior to the Second World War he became a British spy in Germany, narrowly missing being caught by the Nazis.

Recollections from his autobiography 'True Blue' read as follows.

"One day, when I on was on the Hard (at Warsash) with Bevis (the family boatman and driver), we were astonished to see three men-of-war destroyers making their way up the Hamble. They were the escort for the yacht of the last Czar of Imperial Russia, who had come over for the funeral of King Edward VII in May 1910. They had misread their charts, mistaking the Hamble for the Itchen, where they had been built in Thorneycroft's Yard. When they were abreast of Hamble village, they realised their mistake and came out stern first, their propellers churning the muddy waters into brown foam, the strange foreign voices of the leadsmen ringing across the river. I did not appreciate at the time that they were the first foreign men-of-war to come up the river since the days of the Vikings.

"My chief memory of Warsash village, other than the Hard, was Mrs Foy's shop, on what was known as Foy's corner. It had a wonderful smell, compounded of lamp oil, yellow cheese, liquorice, twist tobacco for chewing and Packer's chocolates, which were drops covered with hundred and thousands.

"Tim (J Baker White's stepfather), being a keen yachtsman, used to go over in his motorboat to Bembridge, Bevis at the tiller, myself in the prow. Largely three families, the Mellors, Thorneycrofts and Savilles, ran the yacht club at that time. Roy Saville was one of the best looking men I've ever seen in my life, and along with 'Shuggie' de Bathe and Wilfred Egerton the most immaculate. My picture of the latter is very clear, standing on the landing stage of the yacht club at Bembridge, white-topped yachting cap, stiff white collar with black silk tie and pearl pin, beautifully cut blue flannel double-breasted coat with chalk pin stripe, white flannels with a crease like a knife edge, brown and white shoes, and in one hand a long cigarette holder, in the other a glass of sherry.

"One of the most entertaining was Sir Hugo de Bathe, always known as 'Shuggie'. He acquired a baby Himalayan bear, which he kept in what had been the wash house of the cottage in the garden of Flagstaff in Locks Heath. One day it bit its way round the bars and walked off through the village, causing considerable alarm. A posse of police arrived from Fareham to recapture it; Shuggie packed it off to the zoo.

"I saw a lot of Tom Thorneycroft, who used to take me out in his fast motor boats. He had a special sense of fun. One year he thought Cowes Week seemed rather dull, so he went out into the Roads, poured about fifty gallons of petrol onto the sea and set fire to it. The Captain of the Royal Navy guard ship and the Commander of the Royal Yacht were not amused.

"Another interesting figure on the scene was the late Lord Lonsdale. Regarded by many as a bit of a bounder because of his canary-coloured waistcoats and car, and his outsize cigars, he was blackballed from the Royal Yacht Squadron. The next day its members were horrified to see Lonsdale's yacht flying the biggest White Ensign ever seen off a battleship. The use of the flag is, of course, restricted to the Royal Navy and the Royal Yacht Squadron. The Committee piled into the Club pinnace, and went out to Lonsdale's yacht. Demanding angrily to know the reason for this calculated outrage, they got Lonsdale's smiling reply: 'I'm the Hereditary Lord High Admiral of the Coasts of Cumberland and Westmoreland, and as such am entitled to fly the White Ensign.' The Committee, somewhat put out, retired to consult legal opinion and the College of Heralds. This showed Lonsdale to be right; he was made a member of the Squadron the following year."

In the first half of the 20th century men and women crossed the river to work in the Fairey Aviation factory at Hamble Point. They would leave their many bicycles leaning against the garden wall of Shore House, the present Warsash Sailing Clubhouse. The owner of the house Mr Leney would call in Police Constable Knight, but there was little he could do.

During 1936 several men employed in the construction of AGWI, the predecessor of the Esso oil refinery, would row to Fawley and return each day.

For centuries boat owners have brought their vessels to the Hard to scrape the bottoms, undertake repairs and to recoat with preservative tar or paint. It is recorded that a shipwright named Stephen Penford lived at Warsash in 1727. Some boats were careened, that is laid on their sides as the tide receded. Many had flat wide bottoms and could stand upright, others were fitted with sheer legs that consisted of two sturdy timbers, one each side of the boat and bolted in place. Nowadays there are tall timber piles on the foreshore that vessels can secure to, and maintenance work can be achieved at low tide.

One of the most interesting parts of Warsash history relates to the shipyard situated where the Warsash Sailing Clubhouse now stands. The first owner in 1807 was George Parsons, who earlier had built wooden warships at Bursledon, the most famous being HMS Elephant, Nelson's flagship at the Battle of Copenhagen, where the admiral is reputed to have held his telescope to his blind eye.

The workshops were moved from Bursledon, new houses were constructed in Shore Road for the workers and their families, and an inn named the Shipwright's Arms built at the top of Shore Road. George Parsons' son John moved to Warsash to supervise the business, probably living in the house owned by his father, now named The Anchorage. George died in 1812, with his son and great nephew John Rubie continuing to run the company until 1820, when the latter moved to Southampton.

Evidence of the Warsash yard is clear in the form of large baulks of timber, which formed part of the launchways used when launching a ship. They have been preserved by being immersed in mud alluvium for two hundred years, and have reappeared as the mud receded during the past decade.

The remains of one launchway can be seen situated three metres south of the sailing club jetty, just below the high tidemark. There are three sets of timber approximately seven metres in length, and one and a half metres apart, running parallel to the jetty. The original launchways would have been approximately twice the length of the ship. A second launchway was built approximately fifty metres to the south, with one of its timbers still there. These launchways are clearly shown on an 1836 tithe map.

The ships were constructed with the stern of the ship being a few metres above the high water tidemark. A building named the mould loft was erected on the site, where the drawings, called the lines plan, showing the shape of the hull, were drawn with chalk in full size on the blackened floor. Wooden templates or patterns for the ship's components were then made from the drawings.

These were passed to the shipwrights, enabling them to mark the timber to be used before cutting it to the desired shape and size. Hand tools were used that one does not often see these days: crosscut saws, adzes, drawknives, gouges, wooden planes, some with rounded bottoms, wooden spokeshaves, augers for drilling holes, caulking irons and mallets, to name a few. An adze in skilled hands can cut and remove large pieces of wood quickly when shaping a piece of timber, with the advantage of finishing the work almost to a planed surface.

Tools such as these were still in general use in the local boatyards in 1950 or later.

HRH Prince Charles used the author's adze in 1980 at Southampton to cut a ceremonial rope placed on a wooden block when opening new training workshops for yacht building apprentices. Many of these young persons were employed by companies on the Hamble River.

Prior to the day Prince Charles was due to do his bit for Queen and country, the training centre received a visit from HRH's protection officer. He had been advised that the adze, which is a very sharp tool, should be held high when used, and brought down with a strong blow.

The detective was very concerned that HRH may cut his foot off, and said that

HRH Prince Charles using the author's adze in 1980. By courtesy of the News Portsmouth

he would like to take an adze to London so that HRH could practise. The police officer was shown the safe, easy way to use it, he was a good teacher, and all went well on the day with one short clean cut.

The sawpits in use in the 1807 shipyard were about six feet deep, three feet wide and possibly twenty feet in length. They would have been lined with timber, with a wooden structure built over them with a roof. A trunk of an oak, elm, beech or pine tree would be placed on wooden bearers over the pit, securely fixed in place and sawn into planks. From these planks the ship's components would be sawn, as noted earlier, including the keel, stem, sternpost, the curved frames, the hull and deck planking, and the many beams and knees that hold the structure together. Several hundred trees would be required to build a ship.

The hull planking thickness on these ships was between 75mm and 125mm, the frames or ribs 275mm, plus an inner timber lining of 50mm, forming a very strong structure.

Two men were employed at each sawpit, one standing on the log and the other in the pit below, using a long double-handled pitsaw. This was arduous work considering the thickness and length of the timber. Nevertheless with a sharp saw and sustained effort a considerable amount could be sawn in one day. These types of saws and this method of cutting timber was still being used in the Hamble boatyards in 1950, when large shaped timbers, possibly 400mm in thickness, could not be managed in the modern sawmill. This was generally the task for two apprentices, with the log to be sawn raised onto tall trestles and not in a pit.

Ships built in the early 1800s had only a relatively small number of copper or iron bolts used in their construction, these mainly through the joints in the keel sections, and to secure the frames or in layman's terms the ribs to the keel.

Thousands of round wooden treenails were produced which held the hull structure and planking together in a similar way to dowels. Holes would be drilled into the timbers to be joined and the treenails driven to a very tight fit. These were made of the same timber as the pieces being joined, and in size were from 300mm to over one metre in length and 30mm in diameter.

Each ship took approximately two years to build, with the shipyard owner endeavouring to have two ships under construction at the same time, but at different stages. Craftsmen would then be in continuous employment, and moved from the first ship or back to it as the job demanded. There was the additional advantage that when one ship was completed the yard was still in business with the second.

Four wooden sailing warships were built at Warsash between the years 1807 and 1813.

The Hotspur, 36 guns, was laid down in 1807 and launched in 1810. The Hon Josceline Percy, at 27 years of age, was appointed as her commanding officer. The ship was stationed in the English Channel, with Captain Percy RN, his first lieutenant, William Morgan, and crew leading an extremely heroic life. The ship was in commission for five years before being put into reserve, and then broken up in 1821.

A wooden model replica of Hotspur was made, and presented by ship's carpenter John Chapman in 1827 to the Hon J Percy. This model is now displayed in a glass cabinet in Levens Hall, Kendal, in Cumbria, where it can be viewed by the public.

Another model of Hotspur is displayed in a prominent position in St Mary's Church at Warsash, constructed by the late Commander Peter Clissold RNR, formerly a divisional officer at the School of Navigation.

The next warship built was the Theban, 36 guns, launched in 1810, with Captain S T Digby RN in command, and stationed in the English Channel. She was broken up in 1917.

The Nymphe, 38 guns, was launched in 1812, with Captain F Epworth RN and stationed in America. She later became a hulk ship, that is a store ship, or accommodation vessel for seamen, coastguards or prisoners in 1836.

The Laurel, 38 guns, was launched in 1813, with Captain G Proby RN, and stationed in the Cape of Good Hope in South Africa. She was put out of commission in 1815, eventually becoming a hulk ship.

The dimensions of these vessels were approximately 50 metres in length and 13 metres in beam.

Three of these vessels were in commission with the Royal Navy for a relative short period due to the cessation of the wars with the French and Americans; therefore the ships were no longer required.

When a ship was launched a reception would be held, and persons of note and

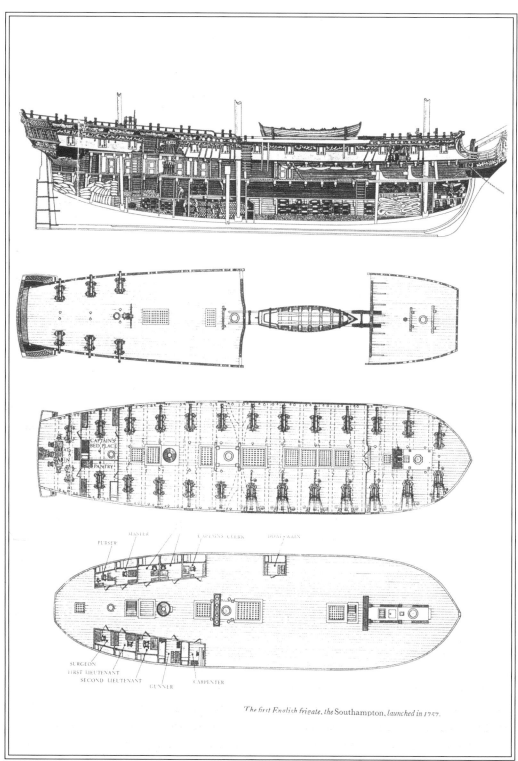

A 32-gun frigate, similar to the four slightly larger 36- and 38-gun warships built in Warsash between 1807 and 1813, illustrated by Ray Woodward

influence invited. The craftsmen would also be entertained later, in their own time, probably on a Saturday evening, with the shipyard owner paying for the beer. Singing at the Shipwright's Arms Inn would have resounded well into the night. These men had certainly earned it while the ship was being constructed, also enduring the arduous working conditions during the winter months.

Ships in Britain were generally built in the open, with the English weather prolonging the construction. In times of war ships had to be built as quickly as possible, so many ships were built with green, that is freshly cut, timber which had not been seasoned. It is much easier to cut, but green timber was a major factor in ships rotting, with costly repairs being required, or the ship being taken out of service. Had the ships been constructed under cover, much of the timber may have seasoned in the dry, during the construction period.

While a ship is being built many problems arise, which may delay completion on time, such as the weather and shortage of craftsmen or materials, in spite of earlier good planning. When this happened the Navy Board imposed very heavy financial penalties, unless the shipbuilder could convince the Board otherwise.

To assist with the preparations and launching of each ship seventy or so shipwrights and riggers would travel from Portsmouth Dockyard to Warsash. Then several days after the great event the warship would be towed to Portsmouth by small boats being rowed by many oarsmen.

There the ship would enter a dry dock to allow copper sheathing to be fitted to the underwater side of the hull to prevent worms attacking the timber. Copper also has the effect of reducing marine weed growth and barnacles, which if allowed to grow would reduce the speed of the ship. The ship would be fitted out with masts, yards, spars, rigging, ropes, sails, anchors, cannons, cannonballs, gunpowder, cutlasses, rifles, boats, furniture, fittings, stores, food, rum, water and the hundreds of items required to keep a ship at sea for several months.

The four warships built in Warsash were classed as 5th rates or frigates. They were not used in the big sea battles, where much larger ships were deployed, such as the 104-gun Victory at Trafalgar, but were used for carrying despatches, escorting merchant ship convoys, undertaking reconnaissance patrols and observing the movements of enemy warships. This class of ship was often involved in skirmishes with the enemy, and captured many French warships and merchant vessels in European waters, similarly capturing Yankee ships off the American coast.

The British officers and seamen received a reward in the form of prize money from the government, the captains of many ships becoming wealthy, with several of these officers buying properties in Warsash. With such an incentive these ships were not in need of the press gang, and volunteers would make up any additional crew required to a total of approximately 220 men. Raids were also made ashore from these ships into enemy territory. The captured ships would be repaired and used by the Royal Navy, generally keeping their original names.

The war with France ceased, and there were no new orders for Parson's yard, although there was still a requirement for many warships to be deployed around the world. The Warsash yard remained open, probably undertaking repairs to merchant vessels, but many craftsmen became unemployed.

Situated on the beach above the northern launchway is a wooden seat, placed there in memory of an early submariner, Engineer Captain George Villar, CBE Royal Navy 1887-1970, also Commodore of Warsash Sailing Club in 1960 and 1961. The seat was made by a Royal Navy shipwright Ron Davidson at HMS Excellent in Portsmouth in 1973.

Continuing on the footpath along the low cliffs, ropes can be seen tied to the branches of oak trees. Children for a century have swung out over the beach here, calling to their parents or grandparents to give them a push.

The next point of interest is near the junction of the shore footpath and Cherry Walk public footpath. The remains of a brick building, now only six courses high, are lapped by sea water at high tide. Several of the bricks are marked Bridgewater, with the building forming part of an early industrial estate.

There is little remaining of the chemical and cement factory which operated here from 1864, or the blast furnace and iron works constructed in 1868. The buildings covered a wide area, where many men were employed. One of the chemical manufacturing processes was the distillation of wood, where timber is heated to produce methanol or methyl alcohol. This produced a residue of charcoal, which had a much higher carbon content than the carbohydrate of the original wood. The charcoal was used

in the blast furnace to produce ingots of iron of a very high quality. Portland cement was also produced, the main ingredients being ground chalk and sea mud.

Redstone machinery base, a surviving artefact from the Warsash chemical and cement works 1864-1882

The chemical works closed in 1882, with the blast furnace stopping production a short time later.

During the summer of 2004 the author searched the wooded area in the grounds of the Warsash Maritime Academy in Newtown Road, hoping to find artefacts remaining from the works, and discovered a large, dressed red sandstone. Its dimensions are over one metre in length, and 450mm by 450mm in width and depth. Two 50mm diameter holes are drilled through it, plus several tooled recesses cut into its surface. It is thought to be part of a machine plinth used during chemical or cement processing, possibly for grinding materials. George Fuller and the author removed the stone after receiving permission from the Maritime Academy. It is now placed in a prominent position, situated on the foreshore between The Rising Sun Hotel and the D-Day memorial.

Until recent years a road led up the hill from the beach. Commencing at the foot of Cherry Walk, it ran through the private garden of Grooms cottage into

Newtown Road. It was originally used by the newly-formed Royal Naval Air Service from 1913 to 1919 and received a tarmac surface.

The RAF also made use of it for vehicles up to circa 1970, with servicemen alighting at the turnaround close to the beach. They would then walk along the path to the pier, and travel by motorboat to the flying boat base at Calshot. There was an additional path here that ran close to the cottage and in the winter of 1947 was used as a toboggan run by children, some coming from Fleet End. These two thoroughfares used by the public were in addition to Cherry Walk.

Adjacent to Grooms cottage were ten hunter boxes, owned by Sir Warden Chilcott, MP until 1942, and used for stabling thoroughbred horses, with harness and tack rooms and a large loft. The trainer, Mr Butler, resided in Grooms cottage. Sir Warden also maintained stables in Upham, near Bishops Waltham.

Sir Warden had purchased the large Hook Park and Warsash Estate in 1911, building a mansion named The Salterns,

now named Admirals House, which can be seen from Cherry Walk footpath.

The estate bailiff, Major Barber, resided in nearby Dorando, now converted to two dwellings named Griffins and Elverhoy.

Continuing along the shore, several new buildings are situated close to the path, replacing Sir Warden's large thatched boat shed and indoor riding school. Behind these buildings stood the head gardener's cottage, occupied by Frank Gibson from 1938 to about 1961. His wife Lillian, from a coal mining village in the Midlands, found ten acres of beautiful gardens with spectacular flower beds, a lake and well-mown lawns sweeping down literally to her doorstep.

Sir Warden did not reside in The Salterns during the Second World War, with the Gibson family moving in as caretakers for approximately two years. Imagine this huge mansion, with lovely views to seaward, with just one family with three very young children.

Back on the shore a narrow creek runs in towards the boathouse, where a pair of metal rails enabled boats to be winched up

Dorando, home of the estate bailiff Major Barber

and placed under cover, where they could be repaired and maintained.

A very long concrete pier here extends well out into the river. It is the third one to be built, the first being erected in 1913 for the Royal Naval Air Service. The officers and ratings were accommodated in the new barracks in Newtown Road, now the Warsash Maritime Academy. The aircraft were built in a factory at Hamble Point, with a wide concrete slipway being constructed for launching the sea planes, which can still be seen from Warsash.

The pier was reconstructed in 1938 and again in more recent years.

To the south of the pier a long line of wooden posts can be seen at low tide in the mud, running parallel with the shoreline.

The posts, now greatly reduced to 200mm or less in height, reinforced the outer soil embankment of a very old saltern, which produced salt from seawater by evaporation, with heat from the sun and air. The salt pans covered an area along the shoreline from the proximity of the present pier to approximately sixty metres from the footpath which leads to the Maritime Academy, and inland to where the land starts to rise. There were internal embankments that formed twenty small bays or pans. Each shallow bay had its own sluice gate which allowed seawater to be let in at high tide, and could be closed as required.

Nature would be left to do its work, with the salt being raked up when the bay had dried out. This process was only carried out during two or three months in the summer. A rainy season meant the resulting brine which had not dried out fully had to be boiled in large metal containers to recover the salt. The uses of salt were numerous, in food and its preservation, and also in a wide range of industrial processes. It is recorded that Giles Rogers was a salt-maker in Warsash in 1745, followed by his grandson, also Giles Rogers, in 1766. These salterns are drawn on an 1836 tithe map.

There were many salterns situated on the Hampshire coast including one at Hamble Point. There was enough salt being produced locally to warrant a government tax collector, called a Salt Officer, to be stationed and housed at Hamble Point. Salterns in France and Portugal are still producing salt in a similar manner today, which is in great demand.

After passing the salterns the path arrives at a tee junction; turning right the path continues on an embankment named Ships Bank, originally built with a stone walled outer face. This was constructed circa 1790 for a former Governor of Bombay, William Hornby. It enclosed the tidal harbour and estuary, and created a non-tidal lake which could be viewed from the mansion, built for Mr Hornby in Hook, close to the existing Golf House.

This sheltered harbour in earlier times had been of great national importance, particularly during the 14th century when Portsmouth was only a small naval port. Eleven ships and over two hundred men sailed from here for Crecy in the year 1346, so it is logical to presume that there would have been repair facilities, with store houses for equipment and provisions.

Buildings and houses are known to have existed in the area, which were cleared to build the new mansion in circa 1788. Most of the former harbour which extended to Fleet End has now silted up, and the small lake remaining is encroached with reeds making an excellent wildlife sanctuary. A new pair of sluice gates has been installed alongside the path, replacing the original 1800 single gate model. A brick tunnel under the footpath, through which water passed, was always good fun for children to clamber through. During the Second World War a dinghy was kept in the wide lake, with children rowing from the sluice gate to the concrete bridge in Hook Park Road, passing the swans' nest on the way.

The next place of interest is Hook Point. This peninsula has been created by the tidal stream, called the long shore drift, that flows along the beach, bringing gravel with it from the cliffs at Chilling. The peninsula has increased enormously in length and width during the past fifty years. The depth of gravel has also increased. The sea wall was 1.5 metres high; now the gravel is level with the top of the wall.

Another Second World War concrete anti-aircraft gun emplacement can also be seen here.

In 1836 a Royal Navy sailing ship, HMS Havoc, built in 1805, was taken into the Coastguard Service and beached in the lee of Hook Point on the shingle bank. Four coastguards and their families lived on board this vessel, where several children were born, and a number of their descendants still reside in Warsash.

Coastguard William Wynhall from Looe in Cornwall was one of these men, with his daughter Jane being born on board in 1843. Jane walked each day from the ship to the school in Hook Park Road, marrying William Gale in 1864, and later residing in Oakbank in Warsash Road.

Another coastguard, William Foy, was born in Ryde in 1824, joining the Royal Navy in 1853, and became a gunners mate. He served as a Coastguard in HMS Havoc from 1873 until 1878. His daughter Harriet was born on board in 1875. She married Austin Hooker, who became the landlord of the Bugle Inn at Hamble. Her brother William was also born in the ship in 1878.

The coastguard's daughter, Jane Newbury, née Wynhall, born on HMS Havoc at Hook Point in 1843

A red brick lifeboat building also stood on the gravel spit at Hook Point, near HMS Havoc.

In 1881 a permanent red brick Coastguard Station was built in Newtown Road, now the site of the Warsash Maritime Academy, with a watch tower, offices and accommodation for eight coastguards and their families. HMS Havoc was acquired by James Lock and renamed The Gypsy Queen. She was beached by the old launchways near The Rising Sun, and used as tearooms in the summer months and for dancing during the winter.

The Royal Humane Society presented the Bronze Medal in 1913 to Walter King of Warsash, aged 15 years, who was one of six children in a small craft that capsized in the creek at Hook Point. He was successful in bringing ashore three of the children; the other two were able to get out unaided.

When standing at Hook Point, all the land that you can see between Hook Point and Solent Breezes at Chilling, and inland to Hook Park Road, was a private golf course during the period circa 1930 to 1943.

It was constructed for Sir Warden Chilcott and used by his many guests, with Warsash youths being employed as caddies. The course fairways were a total of 6,000 yards (5,497 metres) in length, with much of the land previously salt marsh. It was kept dry with surface water draining into wide ditches on the lower perimeters of the course. Mechanical pumps situated in a wooden building nearby discharged the excess water into the lake. The course was designed by leading golf architects, Sir Guy Cambell,

Major Hutchison and Major Hotchkin. Major Hutchison had been one of the designers of Gleneagles.

Prior to the Second World War children collected khaki-coloured pith helmets that washed up on the shore. Soldiers returning in troopships from several years' service abroad in hot climates would throw the unwanted headgear overboard. A white helmet, similar to those still worn by Royal Marine bandsmen, was considered a rare prize indeed.

The author's sons, Mark and Peter, have compiled a list naming the species of fish they have caught off the Warsash coastline during the past five years. Fishing from a boat in the summer of 2004, the following fish were caught in one day: bass, mackerel, red mullet, smoothhound, pouting, bream, thornback ray, eel and a spider crab. Other species previously hooked were cod, flounder, sole, grey mullet, plaice, wrasse, scad, tub gurnard, spurdog, dogfish, whiting, sting ray, small-eyed ray, sunfish, garfish and dabs.

The shell fish clams, cockles, mussels and winkles are found on the beaches, with an occasional crab and lobster.

In 1957 the Caltex Oil Company acquired land in the Chilling and Brownwich areas intending to build an oil refinery. There was a public outcry, with many organisations in opposition to the plan, and eventually the oil company withdrew their application.

We are extremely fortunate not to have lost such a lovely coastline, which is open for all to enjoy, with most of the land being purchased by Hampshire County Council, which should ensure its preservation.

If one is to continue to walk along the shore path past the rabbit warrens you will arrive at the Solent Breezes Holiday Park at Chilling. This venture was commenced in 1946 by Vic Collins and his wife Joan (coastguard Wynhall's great-granddaughter) using some of the ex-army wartime buildings that were on the site. Prior to this there was only a solitary wooden bungalow, mentioned earlier, that stood near the cliff top and owned by Mrs Grant of the whisky distilling family.

A boom defence system to prevent enemy warships entering Southampton Water and the Docks was constructed several years before the First World War in 1911, running from Chilling to Calshot Castle. There were four structures called dolphins in position at intervals across the Water, two built of wood and two of steel, six to ten metres in height, and fitted with small calibre guns. In the event of the boom being required, several old naval ships would be moored stem to stern to form a barrier with strong chains linking each ship and the dolphins. The ships when not in use were moored at Badnam Creek in Bursledon. The boom was dismantled and scrapped in 1921.

In the period about 1960 a tunnel three metres in diameter was constructed under Southampton Water, stretching from Chilling to Fawley, to carry cables for the supply of electricity from the power station to the eastern side of Hampshire. A battery-powered locomotive running on a one-metre gauge railway was used in the tunnel for maintenance purposes for over ten years.

The length of this pleasant coastal footpath from the Ferry to Chilling is approximately two miles, and makes a very enjoyable walk. If one prefers a circular tour there are five public footpaths that lead off the path, at more or less equal distances, therefore making a shorter or varied walk if you wish.

You can return through Newtown Road on the first two paths, through Hook in addition on the next two, finally through Chilling on the fifth. The walker requiring a longer distance can continue on the cliff path or the beach to Brownwich.

The large farm at Brownwich, also part of the Hornby estate, was sold in 1911 with three hundred and sixty acres of land. All the farm buildings, the farmhouse and the four cottages with one third of the land were situated in the parish of Hook with Warsash, the remainder in the parish of Titchfield.

The farmhouse had a large attic on the second floor that was used as a classroom. There was a pump house, with a wheel driven by water conducted from Brownwich Pond, and supplying power for shafting fitted in the barn. This drove a device that turned grain, peas and beans into food for animals, by grinding and milling.

It is interesting to note that in addition to the usual farm buildings, which included a dairy, stables for carthorses, barns, granaries on staddle stones, piggeries etc, there was a large bullock shed for fourteen beasts.

The coastal cliff path continues in open countryside, with sea views to Meon, where the small arable Meon Farm of the Hornby estate, with ten acres, was situated. The two cottages were old and became disused in 1911. Hill Head is only a short distance further.

Newtown and Havelock Roads, from the Clock Tower to the Warsash Maritime Academy

Newtown Road is appropriately named, as at one time it led to the hamlet of Newtown.

A pair of cottages on the eastern side of the road, near the Clock Tower, or Foy's Corner crossroads, was built circa 1910 by Mr Shenley, and sold by auction in 1916. Mr William Harmer and Mr Arthur Stickland were tenants at that time, their annual rent being £26. In 1941, although the tenants had changed, the price of rent for one of these cottages was unchanged.

The founder chairman of Warsash Local History Society, Leila Kroon, resided in the first cottage from 1927 to 1949, her father, Robert Price, being employed as a chauffeur. Leila became a councillor for the Warsash Ward of Fareham Council, and served for twenty-one years.

Havelock Road, named after General Havelock, leads off to the right where there are several interesting cottages. Strawberries and vegetables were cultivated in a large field here up to 1960; there was also a barn owned by Mr Walter Bevis of Rose Cottage.

At the far end of Havelock Road is the imposing Warsash Lodge or Court, with eleven bedrooms, river frontage and excellent views over Southampton Water.

Algernon Sartoris and his wife Nellie, daughter of the American President Ulysses Grant, spent their honeymoon

Warsash House estate workers' cottages in Newtown Road 1916

Warsash Court in Havelock Road, formerly Warsash Lodge

here in 1874. Lord Ellenborough became a resident at a later date, with Sir Ralph St George Claude Gore, Baronet, residing here in 1916. The house was renamed Mainsail Haul for a short period when Admiral Weymss was in residence in 1914.

Returning to Newtown Road, there are several Victorian red brick cottages on the left, named No 1 and No 2 Ann's Cottages, Rose Villa and Lorn Villa. The latter became the residence of James Dickinson, the blast furnace manager, in 1868. On the other side of the road, a block of four cottages once existed, which were demolished in recent years. All eight cottages are shown on an 1870 map.

Continuing along Newtown Road a shop is passed on the left, plus a cluster of Victorian houses. In one of these, named Solent Cottage, resided Mark Spinks, the skipper of Cupid, a crab-carrying ketch. Later Mark became the skipper of the sailing cutter Tally Ho,

owned by Lord Stalbridge of Warsash House, winning the third Fastnet race to be held in 1927. They encountered severe weather, with only two yachts finishing from fourteen starters. Next, laying well back from the road, is the Salterns Working Men's Club. The land was owned by Sir Warden Chilcott, with the building, now extended, being built by Sir Warden in circa 1935 for use by the men of the village.

In 1913 a wooden building stood here, the officers mess for the Royal Naval Air Service, which later moved to the permanent barracks, which is now part of the Maritime Academy in Newtown Road.

Close by stands an attractive cottage which dates from 1720. Research by a previous owner has shown that part of it was most likely built overnight on the common by a squatter. The outer cob walls have since been faced in brick, with extensions that made a terrace of three dwellings, although twenty-five years ago it was all converted into one dwelling.

Three additional buildings once existed close by, shown in a Titchfield tithe map dated 1836. One of these is noted in the 1870 Ordnance Survey map as being a post office, and was one of a pair of cottages that were inhabited during the Second World War. They were demolished in circa 1950 and replaced with a new dwelling in recent years.

On the opposite side of the road to the Club is a very large cream Georgian house named Hamblebank. Walter Greenhill, a Sussex cricketer who played for England in 1868, owned the property in 1875, remaining until his death in 1913. The accommodation was later divided into two dwellings, with Air Commodore Sir Adrian Chamier residing after the Second World War in the apartment now named Farthing House. It is most likely that the stables and cottage for Hamblebank

were in Grooms in Cherry Walk. A connecting path on Hamblebank land is shown on an 1870 map.

In a nearby house resided Rear Admiral Jack Scatchard from 1979 to 2001. He was awarded the DSC for gallantry three times during the Second World War, serving with all the flair associated with a destroyer captain.

After a short distance Queens Road is situated on the left, formerly a footpath called Queens Hill. The white stippled house was built in 1906 as a chauffeur's cottage, with a wooden garage in the garden.

The next older house in Newtown Road on the left is named Forest View, owned at one time by Captain French of the trading vessel Lucretia that often came to the Hamble River.

After a few yards there is a pair of semi-detached cottages, close to the road with cement rendered walls painted white, named Madeira Villas. They were

Hamblebank in Newtown Road, residence of the England cricketer Walter Greenhill (Author)

Note the large well-maintained vegetable gardens between Newtown and Osborne Roads. Photo taken from Madeira Villas in Newtown Road circa 1932, well before the Queens Hill development was constructed

built for James Lock circa 1885 with bricks that had been reclaimed from the old factory buildings near Newtown Road. The bricks had probably been made in a small brickyard a few hundred yards away during the construction of the factory in 1864. Ornate bowed cast iron railings were originally set between pillars on the low wall at the front of the house, but were removed during the Second World War.

In 1908 James Lock's nephew, Henry Woodford, and his wife Jane came from Hamble to live in No 1 Madeira Villas. Their son Ted and his wife Minnie took up residence in No 2 when they married in 1928. Ted and Minnie's son, the author, was born here in 1933, and his sister Gloria in 1941. The cottages had very long gardens which were well cultivated, and fertilised with seaweed carried from the shore in a wheelbarrow.

There was an artesian well in the garden, as with most houses, which was used up to circa 1930 for drinking water. The exterior of the house was regularly painted, with Ted deciding to renovate it again at the age of 84 years. Offers of help were dismissed with comments by Ted that he had spent years on the mast of a square-rigged ship, and on high roofs as a carpenter.

Further on in Newtown Road, on the right, is the driveway into Admirals House. This was the site of the old road originally named The Cutting, leading to the iron smelting and chemical factory mentioned previously.

This blast furnace in the year 1868 was the last one to be built in Britain fuelled by charcoal, a by-product of the chemical works. The author has identified the site of the blast furnace, which is in the grounds of the Maritime Academy. Two

*Ted and Minnie Woodford, née Garman, the author's parents, who were both employed by Sir Warden Chilcott.
The cherub statue stood in The Salterns garden*

large wedge-shaped bricks, with the dimensions 600mm x 300mm x 150mm, which formed the outer wall of the free standing furnace, have been found, one with the wording H Parfit, Firebrickworks, Cwmbran. This company is listed in an 1880 directory as being in business as fire-brick makers at Cwmbran in Wales.

The furnace was built on the side of a hill, with associated iron ore bunkers, and charcoal barns built higher up. The ore and charcoal were placed into a loading floor, with a mixed charge coming out at the other end. The charge was carried over a covered bridge in wheelbarrows, in this case over a road, and into the top of the furnace with no further lifting. The molten iron was run out at the bottom of the furnace into sand moulds. Considerable periods of time would be required between runs, which

were necessary for recharging the furnace. The pig iron was broken into relatively small pieces, which could be carried to a ship lying in the nearby creek, close to the existing modern concrete pier.

Most furnaces during this period used water power to drive the bellows or blowing cylinders, which forced air into the furnace to obtain the high temperatures required. However, there were no streams here, so the machinery would probably have been steam-driven.

Harrison Ainslee and Company operated two other furnaces, one at Newland, near Ulverston in Lancashire, and another at Bonawe on the west coast of Scotland.

Ships carrying iron ore from Ulverston to Bonawe would sail through the Firth of Lorne, hence the works became known as the Lorne furnace. The ingots of good quality pig iron were forged with

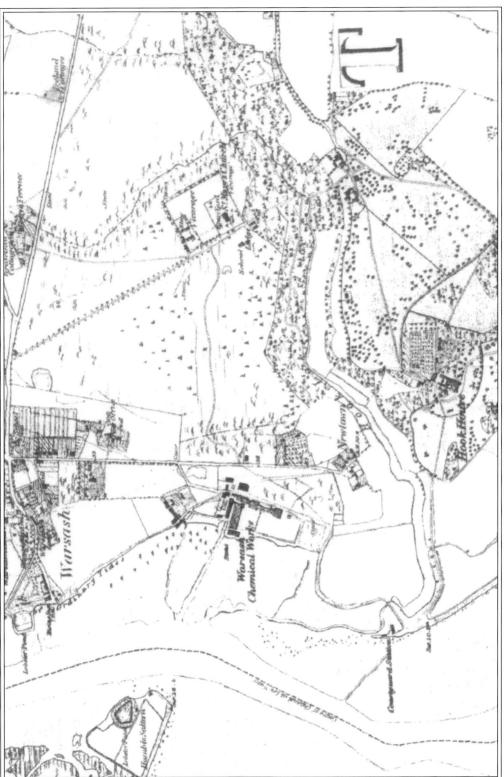

An 1871 map showing Warsash House, the Chemical Works, the Blast Furnace and Hook House. Crown Copyright and Landmark Information Group Ltd

the word LORN, making a trademark that continued at Warsash.

Most of the iron ore used at Warsash was mined in Cumbria and transported by rail to Fareham station, and then by horse and cart to the furnace. The company owned shares in eight ships including the two masted schooners Tom Roper and Warsash. The Tom Roper was built in Barrow in 1857, with the Warsash being constructed at Ulverston by William and John White in 1869. Many deliveries of pig iron were made to their best customer, A Dalifol & Co of Paris, and to a French cutlery manufacturer in Honfleur. On occasions iron ore would be transported by ship from Ireland to the furnaces. The Tom Roper was 120 tons, and 80 feet in length. The smaller Warsash was 58 tons and 72 feet in length, with her first master being James Geldert of Ulverston. During the 1881 census the Warsash was berthed at Ynyscynhaiarn, Caernarvonshire, with another master, Edward Townson, also of Ulverston, Thomas Cross, her mate, and Robert Pinder, an American able seaman from Philadelphia.

The Warsash was destroyed by fire while in Glasgow Docks in 1914, having had a hard working life of 45 years.

In 1882 the chemical works closed, and this affected the supply of charcoal for the smelting furnace. A short time later the Warsash furnace also closed, the manager Mr Dickinson returning to the Newland Works, eventually retiring to Forest View, in Newtown Road, Warsash, where he spent the last fifteen years of his life.

The Bonawe works in Scotland closed in 1876, but has been restored in recent years and is now open to the public.

Mr James Dickinson, manager of the blast furnace that produced pig iron in Warsash

Since those days there have been two other ships with the village name, the first, HMS Warsash, being a Royal Navy Volunteer Reserve Ton class coastal minesweeper, based in Southampton in 1953. A similar vessel was in commission with the Royal Navy Reserve from 1963 to 1968, also based in Southampton. All Royal Navy minesweepers of that class were named when launched after a village with a name ending in 'ton', in these cases Alfriston and Boulston, respectively. When vessels were transferred to the RNVR or RNR they were traditionally renamed with a local connection.

Returning to Admirals House, it is a large, attractive mansion, formerly named The Salterns, built in 1912 for Sir Warden Chilcott, 1871-1942, the Unionist Member of Parliament for the

HMS Warsash, a Ton class coastal minesweeper (Rik Furnival, the Ton Class Association)

Walton division of Liverpool. He served in the Royal Navy Air Service during the 1914-18 war with the rank of Lt Commander, RNVR, became a Justice of the Peace and a Knight Batchelor in 1922, and later served as the Deputy Lord Lieutenant of Hampshire. His interests were in horse racing and yachting. The Salterns had beautiful gardens and lawns, with views across Southampton Water.

Minnie Woodford, née Garman, came to Warsash from her home in Sussex, and became employed as a maid when she was 23 years of age in 1925. She enjoyed working at The Salterns, remarking that Sir Warden was a considerate employer, and would enquire of the maids if they were well fed and happy. They worked long hours and received one day off a week. The house was run in the strict staff

The Salterns, renamed Admirals House

hierarchy of the time, with the butler and housekeeper in command. A host of famous persons including nobility attended the lavish parties arranged by Sir Warden, or Chillie as everyone called him. Guests included the Duke of Westminster, Lord Hewitt, Chief Justice of England, Lord Birkenhead, Lord Beaverbrook, Winston Churchill, Lord Mottistone, Sir Enoch Hill and Lady Hill. Sir Enoch was Chairman of the Halifax Building Society, and conceived the idea of home ownership with mortgage repayments for the masses.

Guests would arrive in light aircraft landing at the airfield in Hook, or travel by car, with chauffeurs sleeping in the rooms above the garage which is now converted into a dwelling named The Coach House.

Sir Warden married Beatrice Baumach in 1896, and although she was alive in 1943 there appears no evidence of her ever living in Warsash. Sir Warden had a good friend, Rosamond Contessa di Sant'Elia.

In her journal on April 1935 the Contessa wrote, "Chillie was mad about politics, his political creed was to maintain justice, cheaper food, less taxation, build houses to provide employment, and a favourite saying, govern us as little as needs be, but govern us when needs be." She travelled with him to the Grand National horse race at Aintree in the grandest style, where his box was one of the best on the course. In her own words she comments that Chillie was very kind and seemed fond of her, he was so good-natured and full of kindliness, that she could not help but be devoted to him, and enjoyed every

moment, with his drive and vitality cheering her up. Later when Chillie was away visiting his castle and demesne in Corsica, and buying a new boat, the Contessa went to a health farm for a cure. The Contessa purchased Springfields, recently enlarged and now known as Kingswood House, a property to the south of Admirals House. The length of time she was in residence is not certain, as in July 1935 she comments that the house had tenants, and when visiting Warsash from her London home she preferred to stay with Sir Warden in The Salterns.

The Contessa also notes that Sir Austen Chamberlain and his wife were installed in their new house next door, known as Red Tiles. This house was later purchased by Sir Warden Chilcott, who leased it to Ralph Richardson. Colonel Clarke bought the house in 1946 and in turn it was sold to Mr George Hampton in 1965 and became the family home for the next twelve years.

Sir Warden had purchased the Hook Park and Warsash Estate in 1911 with 1.25 miles of shoreline frontage and 1,210 acres of land. This included the large Georgian property of Abshot House, Great and Little Abshot Farms, Solent Court Farm, Solent Court Nursery, Hook Park, Grange Farm and in addition a number of cottages.

Sir Warden formed a development company named The Hampshire Estates. Planning approval was obtained for housing, The Salterns, Hook Edge, Rodney's, the Salterns Working Men's Club, a riding school, a boathouse, and a detached cottage was converted into two dwellings, named Sea View, in Newtown Road. The development continued in

Winston Churchill, a guest of Sir Warden Chilcott at The Salterns. National Portrait Gallery, London

The drawing room of The Salterns in 1936, now known as Admirals House, in Newtown Road

The hall in The Salterns in 1936

The chef and butler at The Salterns in 1926

Sir Warden's Hispano Suiza in The Salterns drive

Hook Park with several large houses, an 18-hole golf course, the golf clubhouse conversion, the professional's cottage and the airfield. Sir Warden at this time also owned a farm and stables in Upham, Hampshire, a home in St James Street in London SW1, and a castle and demesne in Corsica. He was born in 1871 and died in 1942. The estate was sold by auction in 1943.

In 1942 during the Second World War the 5th and 12th Commando groups were the occupiers of The Salterns for a short period, followed by the Royal Navy who used it for the remainder of the war as the medical quarters for HMS Tormentor, the combined operations base.

After the Royal Navy had left Warsash in 1946, The Salterns became the residence and office for Captain G W Wakeford, the founder director of the School of Navigation that trained young Merchant Navy deck officer cadets.

Captain Wakeford was a firm disciplinarian; nevertheless he would treat the cadets with kindness and consideration when an occasion arose.

The cadets spent the first year of their training at Warsash before going to sea, each one being interviewed in The Salterns by Captain Wakeford after taking the written entrance examination.

Continuing in Newtown Road, you will find a road on the left named Pitchponds. The Hook harbour estuary came up to the lower area several hundred years ago, so it is most likely that vessels were beached here, their bottoms scraped free of weed and barnacles and recoated. Leaking seams would be caulked with oakum and sealed with hot pitch, boiled in metal containers on the beach, hence the name Pitchponds.

The large complex on the right is the Warsash Maritime Academy. The first buildings to be erected on this site in 1880 consisted of a Coastguard Station with a watchtower and accommodation for eight families. The station was in use until 1913, when it was taken over by the Admiralty.

Many additional brick buildings were constructed, and it became one of the first Royal Naval Air Service stations, the forerunner of the Fleet Air Arm.

In 1917 a Warsash based pilot flew into a 96-metre high wireless mast in fog over Portsmouth. The aircraft became lodged in the metal lattice structure near the top

Cap badge of an officer serving in the Royal Naval Air Service from 1913 to 1918

of the mast, with the unconscious pilot thrown out onto the wing. A naval rating working lower down on the mast with great bravery climbed to the aircraft, bringing the pilot down on his back. In April 1918 the Royal Naval Air Service merged with the Royal Flying Corps to form the Royal Air Force. The barracks were not used after 1919, except for a small part retained by the Household Brigade Yacht Club.

In 1940, during the Second World War, the Royal Navy returned to the barracks, and set up the Combined Services base named HMS Tormentor. Details of HMS Tormentor are written in the chapter Warsash at War.

In 1946 the Royal Navy vacated the base, and it was then taken over by the School of Navigation, now named the Warsash Maritime Academy. Living accommodation and training rooms were

A Royal Navy seaplane, built at Hamble, with the Rising Sun Hotel at Warsash across the river, circa 1917

A light aircraft with pilot lodged in a 96-metre high mast

A view of the Hamble River taken from the premises of the Household Brigade Yacht Club in Newtown Road in 1938

Captain G W Wakeford, MBE, founder director of the School of Navigation, Warsash, in the hall of The Salterns

Captain G W Wakeford in his office at The Salterns, interviewing a prospective cadet candidate

provided for the Merchant Navy cadets. They wore officers' uniform and received instruction in seamanship and navigation, earning the School a very high reputation throughout the world. A radar aerial was installed on the roof of the water tower and used for additional training purposes.

The School, previously based in Southampton, had purchased the 29-metre ketch-rigged Moyana in 1943. She was a wooden sailing vessel, with copper sheathing, of 103 tons Thames measurement, and 49 tons register, built in 1889 by White Brothers of Southampton, originally named the Nereus. Her complement when cruising and training consisted of the master, two officers, the bosun, engineer, cook and fifteen cadets. Her normal cruises were to Lands End, and occasionally to Rotterdam and the Hague.

Garden party at The Salterns for the staff and cadets of the School of Navigation circa 1950

In the summer of 1950, during an office staff day sail, the author's wife climbed to the upper crosstree of Moyana's mast, using the mast hoops for foot and hand hold under the instruction of Bos'un Ferris, whilst at sea off Calshot.

In 1956 the Moyana won the first Tall Ships Race for Britain. Returning from Lisbon, she encountered a storm off the Cornish coast and sank. All the ship's officers, cadets and the trophy were transferred without loss of life to the motor vessel Clan Maclean.

Moyana was replaced with Halcyon, a 78-ton auxiliary ketch, in 1957, in which fourteen cadets at a time could undertake several days' training at sea. The school also owned the 45-ton motor vessel South Hill, which was used for training with radar equipment, and later the ex-motor yacht Somerset.

There was a parade ground in the barracks where the cadets carried out marching drills. They were also sent to HMS Excellent in Portsmouth for training with small arms and the Bofors gun. Many of these Merchant Navy officers in later years returned to Warsash to undertake courses and certification for advancement to senior positions.

The Duke of Edinburgh often came to Warsash by car from 1948 to 1950, leaving his Bentley at the School of Navigation before proceeding to Cowes and sailing with Uffa Fox.

HRH Prince Charles came here in 1975, as the Commodore of the Royal Thames Yacht Club, attending the Club's bicentenary ball at the College of Maritime Studies, now named Warsash Maritime Academy.

Training Ship Moyana, winner of the first Tall Ships race in 1956. Crewed by the officers and cadets from the School of Navigation, Warsash

Aloft on the mast at sea in the sail training vessel Moyana

The School of Navigation's radar training vessel South Hill on the slipway leading into the School's workshops adjacent to the concrete pier

The School of Navigation's training vessel Somerset

Lord Louis Mountbatten inspects the cadets from the School of Navigation, Warsash circa 1951

HRH Prince Charles, as Commodore of the Royal Thames Yacht Club, attending the club's bi-centenary ball at the College of Maritime Studies, Warsash on 25th July 1975, accompanied by the college director, Captain Chris Phelam. Picture courtesy of Southern Daily Echo

HRH Princess Margaret on one occasion flew in by helicopter, en route to a ceremony regarding a yacht at Swanwick.

Rt Hon the Countess Patricia Mountbatten of Burma visited the Maritime Academy in March 1989 to open the new library.

The buildings constructed for the coastguards and the Royal Navy have been replaced with the exception of one building, now named Coastguard.

Across the road is a terrace of four cottages known as Daisy Bank, built for James Lock circa 1885.

To the left of the cottages a gravel lane leads to a house named Withybank. It is an old building with part of it dating from the 17th century. Philly Coombs has resided in this house with his wife Ann and family since 1960. This area at one time formed the hamlet of Newtown, with a quay and a ferry to Hook.

Returning to Newtown Road, a footpath runs alongside the Maritime Academy which leads to the shore footpath and Ships Bank.

Newtown Farm, seen on the right, may date back to the 18th century, with a small thatched barn close to Newtown Road that continues over a bridge into Hook Park.

Warsash residents circa 1900, Mrs Sandy, Mrs Birch and Mrs West

The Coastguard Station in Newtown Road circa 1900

Hook Park, commencing at the Warsash Maritime Academy and continuing to Workmans Lane

The bridge between Hook Park and Newtown Road circa 1946, with the former School of Navigation buildings, now the Warsash Maritime Academy, in the background

The road into Hook Park crosses the estuary, now known as Hook Lake, over a concrete bridge. In early times a rowed ferry was used, but as the harbour silted up a narrow wooden pedestrian bridge was built. It was still being used with care in 1944. Another bridge, suitable for horses, was built by Sir Warden Chilcott in his early days in Warsash. This was replaced with a wide bridge in circa 1930, with elegant stone balustrades on each side of the bridge's length. The bridge was rebuilt in recent years, but the balustrades were not replaced.

A point of interest after crossing the bridge is the remains of an ice house. A lane turns to the left, with the ice house situated approximately thirty metres past the wooden gate, and ten metres to the left, in the trees. It was constructed circa 1790 for use by the Hook House staff, later neglected, and discovered in 1943, virtually intact except for its entrance tunnel and wooden door. Originally six metres deep and three metres in diameter, it was built in brick with a domed roof, topping at about one and a half metres above ground level, and covered in soil and vegetation for insulation. Ice would be cut from the lake or ponds in the winter and packed into the ice house, laid on straw with a layer of straw on top, and could remain frozen for over one year. It was built into a bank in order that a drain could be fitted in its base to carry away meltdown water. The ice house was not used for the preservation of food, but to keep drinks and confections made in the kitchen cool. In recent years the roof has collapsed, but it is still worth a visit.

In the spring of 2005 a badger was trapped in the now two-metre-deep ice house. An RSPCA Collection Officer tried to retrieve it from a burrow in the rubble but it was difficult to reach, and cat food left overnight was not the answer. Honey sandwiches were placed by the burrow the following day, and overnight the badger ate the food and walked to safety on the wooden boards that had been laid in the pit. The Nature Reserve Rangers have now placed several tree trunks with branches to form a ladder that will prevent further incidents.

It is on record that a chapel existed in Hook, close to the water and used by seamen, dating back to the 14th century. The nearest church otherwise was at Titchfield. Clues to the chapel's existence are yew trees, growing in a place several hundred yards along the path, overlooking the steep old harbour bank. A building situated at about this position is drawn on an 1870 Ordnance Survey map.

The earlier village of Hook, its name derived from the hooked-shaped harbour entrance, was much larger than the combined hamlets of Warsash and Newtown. Buildings and houses are known to have existed near the ferry landing, and cleared before Hook House was built circa 1788.

The first house on the right-hand side of the road is named Sunburst, where Sir Maurice Jenks, Lord Mayor of London in 1931, resided from 1932 to 1940. He owned a motor cruiser named Lady Christabelle, which was one of the first motor yachts built by A H Moody and Son of Swanwick in 1938.

On the left at the top of the hill is the red brick Golf House, now converted into apartments.

To the seaward side of Golf House, with panoramic views over Southampton Water, once stood the palatial mansion named Hook House, built during the years 1786 to 1788 in the Palladian style of architecture for William Hornby, a former Governor of Bombay from 1771 to 1783. The house was built mainly with bricks, with impressive Portland stone pillars on the ground and first floors of the façade and entrance, with its appearance similar to Government House in Bombay. A very elegant conservatory, eleven by six metres, was also constructed and is still in existence, although unfortunately it now has a flat roof.

There were two carriage drives, one from Warsash, the other from Hook. The former passed by St Mary's Church, then over a picturesque stream flowing through a pretty wooded gulley, afterwards converging with the approach from Hook Village, winding through the park to the main entrance gates, which were guarded by a pair of white brick-built entrance lodges, one on each side of the road, situated at the Cowes Lane crossroads.

Expansive lawns surrounded the whole south west front of the mansion, and were effectively laid out with finely grown clumps of rhododendrons. Other ornamental shrubs were nicely shaded by specimen and timber trees. Shrubbery walks led from the front lawns to the pleasure gardens, tastefully arranged and surrounded by trees, including araucaria, deodara, cupressus, evergreen oak and yew.

Hook House, seat of William Hornby Esquire, formerly the Governor of Bombay from 1771 to 1785, constructed in circa 1790 and destroyed by fire in 1903

The estate, with 1,495 acres of land and approximately three miles of shoreline, had been purchased from the Duke of Portland in 1783. It included the five capital corn and stock farms of Hook Grange, Green Lane, Great Chilling, Brownwich and Meon.

Additional buildings were constructed, including a coach house, stables, a walled kitchen garden, cottages, the school, a dairy, the laundry, gamekeeper's cottage, also the wheelwright's, carpenter's and blacksmith's cottages and workshops. Most of the buildings are intact except for the dairy and its nearby cottages, and the gamekeeper's cottage.

Fifty acres of the estate were woodland and used for shooting; there were marshes adjoining the lake where snipe and wild fowl could be found.

William Hornby died in 1803 with the house and estate being inherited by his son John, then passing on to members of the family for the next century.

An engraving was made in 1859 by James Gray featuring twelve different buildings in the Hornby estate. These were Little Abshot Farm, Hook Grange Great Chilling, Hook House, its conservatory and gate lodges, Fish House, the cottage named Trivetts, Hook Cottages, Brownwich Farm, the Dairy House and the School House in Hook Park Road. The original block is still in use, with printed copies being produced.

During the evening of 17th July 1903, at a time when extensive renovations were being carried out, a fire started in the house. It spread rapidly until only a few outside walls remained standing, burning literally to the ground.

The estate was inherited by the Hon Albert Hood, who in 1911 gave instructions that it was to be sold by auction by James Harris and Son,

An engraving of Hook House circa 1859

Hook House viewed from Hook Point, with the lake and Ships Bank in the foreground.
From an engraving by James Gray 1859

The coat of arms of William Hornby Esquire of Hook Park

auctioneers of Winchester, the sale to take place in the Dolphin Hotel in Southampton, unless it was previously disposed of by private contract.

Mr H Mortimer purchased Chilling and Brownwich farms, and Fish House, renting out Chilling and Fish House and living in Brownwich himself. The Meon farms were sold separately, with Sir Warden Chilcott buying the remainder of the estate.

Golf House, mentioned earlier, is the former coach house to Hook House. The Contessa on 23rd July 1935 wrote of its conversion:

"The old Georgian facade was left practically untouched, except for removing the huge doors with rounded tops, designed for the passage of the horse-drawn family coaches, and replaced

with great windows. The large portico with round pillars and the front door in the centre of the building were transferred from the entrance of Hook Grange. The interior had been transformed, with an entrance hall, lounge, dining room, card room and bar, all tastefully furnished. The total cost of the conversion was £2,000, with Sir Warden and myself being involved in the planning. We were very proud that this had become one of the most charming golf houses in the South of England."

A professional's shop and cottage were built to the north of the building. A dormy house was also constructed.

The Contessa also noted that Lord Mottistone, the Lord Lieutenant of Hampshire, and his daughter Katherine came to lunch in The Salterns on that day. He was very lively, with a good political career, and a favourite at the Court. During the afternoon they all visited Golf House that was very much admired.

These buildings originated from the Hornby estate, with a clock and bell which struck the hours situated on the roof of the stable. There was also a brew house nearby.

A walled garden that extended to over two acres behind Golf House included two greenhouses with heating systems. The garden was rented by Mrs Atkinson in 1908, where she built up a market garden business including a large orchard. She lived in the bungalow on Chilling Cliff. After the 1914 to 1918 war Mrs Atkinson arranged a training scheme in the Hook Park gardens for ex-servicemen, who for health reasons needed to be in the countryside, or for those who wanted to take up a career in horticulture. Mr Fred Fuller was one of these persons, who had been living in London after being injured in the war. He came to Hook and found he enjoyed the horticultural life, working and residing here for the rest of his life. The huge walls surrounding the garden still exist, built of red brick in the attractive traditional English bond, standing three metres in height, approximately 74 metres in length on each of two sides and 120 metres on the third, and appearing to be in good condition after 200 years.

After passing several modern houses one arrives at the Cowes Lane crossroads. The gate and gatekeeper's lodge for Hook House once stood here, built with bedrooms on one side of the road and living rooms on the other. Turning to the right is Workmans Lane, where on the right hand side stood the imposing and substantial Georgian four-storied house, Hook Grange. There were eight bedrooms, with two staircases to the first

floor and a large cellar. It was built in 1740 and fitted with bells to call the servants. Water for use in the house was pumped up by hand from a well. Behind the house stood a dairy farm with stalls for cows, loose boxes, a cattle shed, stables, harness room, coach house and a granary on staddle-stones. There were stalls for sixty-six cows, with milking commencing at 3.00 am each morning. The cows grazed in fields near the shore, hence the name Cow Lane, later to become Cowes Lane. The farm lands consisted of over three hundred acres, of which one hundred and fifty acres were rich pasture. Hook Grange became disused and was demolished after the Second World War.

On the eastern side of the road, encompassing a very large area, was Sir Warden's private grass airfield. It stretched from Cowes Lane crossroads to

Hook Grange in Hook Park, built in circa 1740, demolished in circa 1950

An engraving of Hook Grange in Hook Park by James Gray, dated 1859

Beam Cottage in one direction, and a greater distance to the east. The aircraft with the registration G A CLZ is a De Havilland DH 85 Leopard Moth owned by Mr W G Robson, and was flown from Heston airfield near Heathrow during the years 1934 to 1936.

An aerial photographic view of the airfield is included, with eight aircraft, taken in circa 1935.

The persons using this airfield were guests of Sir Warden's, either in his home at The Salterns in Newtown Road, or playing golf at the nearby links, with the club house only 400 metres from the airfield.

Sir Warden Chilcott's private airfield in Hook Park in 1935. Hook Grange and the trees in Workmans Lane can be seen in the top left of the photograph, with Southampton Water in the background

Close up view of the guests' aircraft

A De Haviland DH 85 Leopard Moth aircraft in Hook Park airfield circa 1935, owned by Mr G Robson and flown from Heston airfield near Heathrow during the years 1934 to 1936

⊰ HANTS. ⊱

ON the Solent, at the junction of the River Hamble with Southampton Water, immediately opposite Calshot Castle, 3 miles from Swanwick Station on the Netley Branch of the L. & S. W. Ry., 8 miles from Southampton, 4 miles from Fareham, and 10 miles from Portsmouth.

Illustrated Particulars with Plans and Conditions of Sale

OF THE

Important and Valuable Freehold Property

KNOWN AS

THE HOOK HOUSE ESTATE,

EXTENDING TO AN AREA OF ABOUT

1495 acres,

HAVING A

SEA FRONTAGE OF UPWARDS OF 3 MILES to the Solent and Southampton Water

AND INCLUDING THE

Site of the Residence "Hook House"

(Recently destroyed by fire), for many years the seat of the Hornby Family, occupying an unequalled position amidst Grandly Timbered Pleasure Grounds and Parks, with Extensive and Beautiful Views of the Isle of Wight (including Osborne and Cowes) and over the New Forest,

Offering a Grand Site for the Erection of an Up-to-date Mansion, with Grounds already made.

Five Capital Corn and Stock Farms,

having exceptionally good Residences and all let to substantial Tenants (the Sporting being reserved).

Compact Small Holdings & Accommodation Lots

of 6 to 40 ACRES.

Building Sites, Wheelwright's Shop & Land, Smith's Shop & Premises,

BLOCKS OF WELL-BUILT COTTAGES, GARDEN GROUND, &c.

WHICH

Messrs. JAMES HARRIS & SON

Have been honoured with instructions from the Hon. ALBERT HOOD, to Sell by Auction, at

THE "DOLPHIN HOTEL," SOUTHAMPTON,

On MONDAY, SEPTEMBER 18th, 1911, at 2.30 o'clock precisely.

(Unless previously disposed of by Private Contract.)

Particulars with Plans and Conditions of Sale may be obtained at the place of Sale; of MESSRS. PYKE,

Sale of the Hook House Estate, September 1911

Shore Road, from the Clock Tower to the Rising Sun Public House

The crossroads at Warsash circa 1902 prior to the Clock Tower being built

As its name suggests, this road leads to the Hamble River.

In 1903 tall trees overhung the wall and road where Roxby Garage now stands. To the south, at the junction with Newtown Road, Miss Fanny Gregory ran the grocer's shop in a building named Prospect Place, with her surname over the door being changed to Foy after her marriage.

At about that time Mr George Shenley, the American owner of Warsash House, built the Clock Tower with the adjoining coach houses, stables and harness rooms.

Three large metal tanks were built into the top floor which supplied water to the mansion and the immediate estate. A most unusual Gillett and Johnson clock with a large bell was installed, which struck ship's time. A gilded sailing ship weathervane was mounted on top of the tower, and an engraving of a prancing horse on the west wall completed the picture. A trap door in the roof opened onto a viewing platform. The tower is of good architectural appearance and provides a landmark.

A generator produced electricity for lighting Warsash House, the gardens, the Lodge and the Clock Tower buildings.

The buildings adjoining the Clock Tower, where the chauffeurs, coachmen and their families lived, were also used to garage the range of beautiful cars which Mr Shenley owned. A small hexagonal brick building with a tiled cap still exists to the west of the tower, being originally used as a petrol store.

One entrance to these facilities and the Tower was from Shore Road. Tall pillars

The view of the Clock Tower from the west circa 1930

Engraving on the west side of the Clock Tower above the arch (Author)

The Clock Tower with its surrounding wall in the snow

The Clock Tower circa 1952

Mr George Shenley's motor vehicles circa 1907 behind the west side of the Clock Tower in Warsash

surmounted with ornate wrought ironwork and elaborate electric lamps stood either side of wooden gates, with one pillar still standing.

In 1934 Mr Victor Collins, a very successful motor cycle speedway rider, son of the Warsash butcher, purchased the Clock Tower. He demolished the tall wall on the road boundary, and built a modern motor vehicle repair and service station with electric petrol pumps. The water tanks were removed from the tower, the arches on the ground floor bricked up, and the building converted into a dwelling for Vic, as he was known, his wife Joan and daughter. The coach houses were converted into shops, with brickwork being removed and replaced with windows overlooking Shore Road.

In circa 1920 Foy's shop was sold to Mr Fox, who kept it well stocked, also selling beers and spirits and providing a delivery service, albeit a boy with a bicycle.

In the adjoining house, No 1 Prospect Cottages, resided Mr and Mrs Peckham, with Mrs McCall in No 2, who sublet her front room to Martin's Bank for a few hours per week.

Their immediate neighbours were Mr Charlie Fuger and family. Charlie ran a bus service from these premises in 1925, with regular services to Swanwick toll bridge and Fareham, and a daily service to London. Fierce competition arose from the two much larger bus companies, the Southdown and the Hants and Dorset, who owned newer and larger vehicles. There were often races between competing buses to get to the next stop and pick up the waiting passengers. Charlie was eventually obliged to sell out to the Hants and Dorset in 1936.

Charlie Fuger's bus circa 1930

Details of Mr Fuger's company are recorded in Frank Claxton's very interesting book 'Up with the Blues and Down with the Greens', which also includes the commercial vehicles and private cars being used in Warsash from 1920.

The Fuger family have resided in Warsash for many generations. Henry Fuger came from Milton in Hampshire, marrying Rossetta Bevis, who was born here in 1828. Their first son Henry was born in 1852, followed by William, Thomas, Mary, James and Harriet. The four men and their numerous male descendants have been employed as fishermen or yachtsmen, some with their own fishing vessels, or as members of the crew in deep sea merchant ships.

At about the time of the bus company closure Mrs Fuger opened a small grocer's shop, which later became a café and ice cream bar, ably assisted by her five daughters in turn as they grew up. The café became a meeting place for the youths of the village in 1948.

Young persons could not enter pubs before the age of eighteen. There were no pub meals for the family in those days. Generally speaking women did not go to a public house on their own or in a group, only if accompanied by their husbands or male friends. It was also considered not etiquette for a woman to go to the bar to buy drinks.

In their leisure time the village youths played football, cricket and tennis in the recreation ground, with visits by bus to the cinemas in Southampton or Fareham and on occasions to see live shows in the theatres in Portsmouth and Southampton. Lessons in ballroom dancing in Southampton stood them in good stead at dances. These were held in the Victory Hall and other local village and town venues, including the trendy Tower ballroom on the seafront at Lee-on-the-Solent. Sea angling from the beach and boats throughout the year was always popular, and of course the fish were bigger then. A diving board with a good spring to it was built by teenagers over the deep water creek at Hook Point; they also went swimming in the large open-air lidos in Southampton and Hilsea at Portsmouth.

A visit to the New Forest, Romsey or Winchester were all within a day's cycle ride. There was a considerable amount of kudos to be gained if a person owned a bicycle manufactured by Claude Butler, Dawes or Rotrax.

The motor cycle speedway stadium in Southampton was also well supported. The working week at that time was forty-four hours, which generally meant being at work on Saturday mornings, or in the summer working from 7.30 am to 5.30 pm for five days each week. The annual holiday entitlement had recently been increased from one to two weeks.

The sport of youth cycle speedway swept the country, with the Warsash lads racing on a circular track in Thornton Avenue, and occasionally competing with lads from other villages. One half was on a concrete surface and the other on gravel, taking in the road and track that encircled the clump of chestnut trees.

They were all waiting to be conscripted into the armed services for two years' National Service from the age of eighteen or deferred to twenty-one for apprentices.

George Fuller and his Norton 500cc motorcycle in 1953

The majority of young men were required to serve in the Army or Royal Air Force, with a few joining the Royal Navy. Men serving in the Merchant Navy were exempt, providing that they remained in the Merchant Navy until the age of twenty-six years. Philly Coombs, who had been called for National Service several years earlier at a time of a national fuel shortage, was required, instead of being enlisted in the armed services, to work for over three years in a coal mine in County Durham.

One of his jobs was controlling the pit ponies which hauled the underground coal wagons from the coal face to the lift shaft. A government minister, Ernest Bevan, had instigated this scheme; therefore the young men working in the pits were called Bevan boys.

Young women were not required to undertake National Service.

A little further in Shore Road on the right is a pair of attractive red brick cottages named Tumbleweeds and Robin Hill. An 1837 tithe map shows that a building existed here at that time. It was formerly a terrace, with four families in residence in 1916, and owned by the Warsash House Estate. The tenants were Messrs Scrivens, Osman, Barry and Frogbrook. The rents were three shillings per week for the first two named, with the latter two cottages being rent free, as the tenants were estate workers.

The Haven, a property of larger proportions also owned by the estate, lay opposite, but was to be demolished in 2005.

On the southern side of the road, in earlier times, stood the Shipwright's

Arms public house, next to a blacksmith's workshop, both built in 1807 during the shipbuilding days.

The author's grandmother, Jane Woodford, recalled the village men often going to the Shipwright's Arms for a drink at lunch time, circa 1890. They occasionally stayed longer, drinking and singing all afternoon. The employers became exasperated because work was not being done, the wives furious as there would be little money on pay-day, and Mr Sartoris, the owner of Warsash House, annoyed because of the noise. So he bought the pub and closed it down.

There was then only one pub in Warsash for the next sixty or seventy years, apart from the Jolly Farmer in Fleet End, compared to six in Hamble.

This situation remained until the Silver Fern opened in circa 1960, and Great Harry, now The Ferryman, following in circa 1966.

The next older house on the left with its walls standing up to the road is Warsash Court, or Lodge, its main entrance in Havelock Road. A high bank at one time followed the road almost to the river, with tall elm trees growing along its length.

A detached residence named Stone Cottage, with a stone garden wall, is situated at the junction with Passage Lane.

A row of cottages on the right-hand side follow, leading to The Rising Sun. The first one is built of stone and named The Anchorage. It is recorded that a farmhouse stood on this site in 1525, backed up with evidence from an Elizabethan map which can be seen in the archives at Winchester, the remaining houses having been built later, some in 1807 for the shipyard workers, with additions in 1864 when the chemical works were under construction. The

The Haven in Shore Road situated opposite Tumbleweeds was demolished in 2005 and replaced with new dwellings

The blacksmith's workshop in Shore Road, adjacent to the Shipwright's Arms

THE VILLAGE BLACKSMITHS.

The village blacksmiths

The junction between Shore Road and Passage Lane circa 1900

The Bungalow in Shore Road in 1916, renamed Stone Cottage

building next to The Rising Sun was built as a store house, with large doors on the ground floor, wide enough for a horse and cart to pass through. There were double doors and a gantry on the first floor.

Several of the houses in the terrace here were used as tea rooms during the crab and lobster days.

At the foot of the hill on the right stands The Rising Sun. On the left the Warsash Sailing Club, formed in 1957, also overlooks the river. The building has been in use by the club since 1979, and extended in recent years. It was originally named Dock Cottage; nowadays it is known as Shore House.

Dock Cottage, Stone Cottage, The Anchorage and The Watch House were all part of the Warsash House Estate up to 1916.

Further evidence of the Fuger family is shown in 1916, with Thomas Fuger renting The Watch House and the cottage next door. John Bucket rented The Anchorage with a rent of £7 per year. They also shared a rented boathouse, near the river, which was demolished in 2004, and a house built in its place. Behind the cottages at that time stood a commodious coal merchant's business, with a storage shed and office, and a well for obtaining water.

In 1858 Lt Col Dugmore owned the 8.3-metre long racing cutter Sorella, built by Dan Hatcher of Itchen Ferry in Southampton. She was later purchased by William Fuger and used as a fishing boat. In turn she passed down through the Fuger family, eventually being sold and restored in 1983 by Mr Chris Waddington of Wicormarine in Porchester. She proved to be a fast vessel and was purchased from Mr Waddington by an Italian.

Shore Road circa 1910

Shore Road circa 1910

Circa 1954 The Rising Sun Hotel and the Clock Tower

The author and friends 1961
(left to right: John Rowe, boat builder; Ray Cox, precision engineer; Roger Humby, Merchant Navy deck officer;
Don Paul, yacht builder; Bryan Woodford, author, Royal Navy CPO shipwright artificer;
Stan Goodenough, yacht yard accountant; Bob Abrams, boat builder; Ken Cole, painter and decorator)

Dock Cottage, built in 1906 by George Shenley, now known as Shore House. Home to John Dickinson 1906,
Walter Leney 1908, Royal Navy Engineering Officers including yachtsman Alec Rose during the Second World War,
Royal Thames Yacht Club circa 1947 and the Warsash Sailing Club in 1979

Bill Fuger with the racing cutter Sorella, built in 1858, which was owned and used by his family for fishing for over 120 years. The vessel was restored by Chris Waddington of Wicormarine in Porchester in 1983. With courtesy of The News, Portsmouth

Charles Fuger, boatman to the Royal Thames Yacht Club in 1956, later to be appointed as the captain of a 30-metre ocean-going motor yacht

Tom Cozens, Hamble River Harbourmaster 1938 to 1972, who resided in Greenaway Lane, Warsash. Commodore of Warsash Sailing Club 1959 and 1960

Three yachts named Xarifa

Xarifa is an Arabic word for a Charming Lady.

John Dickinson, the son of James Dickinson, the Warsash blast furnace manager, gained his certificate in navigation in 1902. He was appointed as the navigator in the 1,800-ton steam yacht Triad which moored at Warsash, owned by Mr George Shenley, an American residing in Warsash House.

John Dickinson, Captain of the three yachts named Xarifa

In 1906 James Lock retired and sold his crab and lobster business to John Dickinson and Mr Shenley, with John becoming the manager. Mr Shenley, a very wealthy person, arranged for Dock Cottage to be built, now the Warsash Sailing Club, as a residence for John and his family.

In 1912 Camper and Nicholson of Gosport built and launched the ketch Xarifa, a large sailing vessel, 34 metres or more in length. She was owned by Franklin Singer, son of Isaac Singer the sewing machine inventor and manufacturer. John Dickinson was appointed as the captain, and Ted Pannell, also from Warsash, became a member of the fourteen crew.

John and his wife Elizabeth, née Woodford, built a house in Newtown Road, Warsash, naming it Ruby Villa after their daughter, and raised six children. Ted Pannell during part of his married life also lived in Newtown Road in Rose Cottage, later moving to Osborne Road.

The next Xarifa was a three-masted schooner built for Franklin Singer by Samuel White in Cowes; John Dickinson was again the captain with Ted Pannell in the crew, later becoming the navigator.

It is of interest to note that the schooner Xarifa was used in the many 1950s films with Hans and Lotte Hass in their underwater diving adventures.

The third Xarifa for Franklin Singer was a steam yacht of 800 tons, also built by Samuel White in 1932. John Dickinson was again appointed as the captain, with Ted Pannell serving as second officer and navigator. On one voyage to the Far East this ship travelled 19,000 miles. Both men occasionally came home by air, on the ship's business and leave.

The yacht owner once gave John three hundred pounds for safely bringing a compass back to England. Ted invariably spent some of his time, when in Britain, racing Dragon class yachts in Scotland.

There were 40 persons in the Xarifa crew, including local men Barney Woods,

Three yachts named Xarifa

The ketch Xarifa, launched at Gosport in 1912, with HMS Victory afloat in the background

Ruby Villa, the residence of John and Elizabeth Dickinson in Newtown Road

Wally Bevis, Tom Fuger, Fred Arnold, Tom Edwards and Lionel Jefferies.

When the Second World War was declared, the Xarifa was in the Mediterranean Sea. She was escorted by the Royal Navy to Northern France before crossing the English Channel on her own, and returned to England. As the yacht was owned by an American it was requisitioned by the United States government for war service, and converted into a hospital ship.

The third Xarifa 1932

Warsash Road, commencing at the Clock Tower, to Fleet End

Warsash Road, originally named Titchfield Road, runs from the Clock Tower to the junction with Hunts Pond Road and Common Lane, which is only a short distance from Titchfield Village. The road runs for its entire length of two miles through land which at one time formed Titchfield Common. Therefore, this would be a good time to describe the boundaries of the Common before Parliament passed the Common Enclosures Act in 1864.

The boundaries were not straight, but to give an indication of the size I will describe it as forming a triangle, joined to a rectangle.

Commencing at the Clock Tower with the Warsash Road as one side of the triangle, continue towards Titchfield, turning left into Hunts Pond Road, then to Park Gate, and left again into Brook Lane, returning to the Clock Tower.

In addition, it took in a rectangular area where Fleet End, St Mary's Church, Pitchponds Road and Newtown Road are now situated, and their back lands, including the land down to the shore, where the chemical works were to be built. There was also a considerable amount of common to the north of Sarisbury and Park Gate. The Common consisted mainly of moorland with gorse, heather, bracken and trees and with some grazing areas. Local people were able to put their horses, donkeys, pigs and cows out to feed, and to find wood and heather turf for use as fuel for cooking and heating, but this was not possible after the enclosures. The aim of the Enclosures Act was to provide additional land throughout England for cultivation, and to provide food for the increasing population.

The wealthy landowners whose estates surrounded the common were given the land, the rich becoming richer and the poor poorer. Most of the land was eventually sold to local people, who in general bought it in small four- or five-acre plots. If you live in the areas mentioned, look at the deeds of your own land or property, where you may see one of these estate owners mentioned. Three of these were Quintin Hogg, father of Lord Hailsham, who resided in Holly Hill mansion at Sarisbury, Mr Sartoris of Warsash House and Mr Hornby of Hook House.

By 1920 most of the ex-common land was under cultivation with strawberry plants, encompassing half of Warsash, all of Fleet End and the new villages of Locks Heath and Titchfield Common. There were only a relatively small number of houses built, which included the strawberry growers' homes.

On the southern side of Warsash Road is The Ferryman public house, originally named Great Harry, and licensed in 1966. It was originally a private house named Binfield, forming part of the Warsash Estate. Miss Caroline Swinton lived here, and in 1852 opened a school in the house for the village children. The school continued for forty-one years. The school house received an electricity supply for lighting in 1903 with power generated in the Clock Tower buildings. Most dwellings at that time had only oil lamps and candles.

The house named Binfield in 1916, now The Ferryman public house

The head gardener's cottage in Warsash Road

Warsash Road, near the Reading Room

The Reading Room and War Memorial in Warsash Road

The first house on the left, built in 1906 by the Warsash House Estate, was a pretty residence for the head gardener, with its water supply coming from the Clock Tower reservoir. It was sold in 1916, and in circa 1930 became the home of Mr Skilton, the headmaster of Sarisbury Senior School, now Brookfield School, with a tall monkey-puzzle tree in the garden. Further on is the Silver Fern public house, which has been in existence since circa 1960, its name derived from the national emblem of New Zealand, the first landlord and his wife being Kiwis. A much different building was here in 1930, named Oakley's Café, which was used as a WVS canteen in the Second World War, and tearooms again after the war.

The Village Reading Room was built in 1885, followed by the Victory Hall in 1926. The interlinked buildings were regularly used as a meeting place by many organisations, and as a dance hall. All that remains of these buildings is a finial from the roof which is displayed in the newer village hall.

A memorial was erected here in 1919 after the First World War for 28 young men who had died, and in 1945 a plaque was added for the sixteen men who did not return after the Second World War.

In early 1951 Mr George Ellis, a dentist, and his wife Ruth came to work

Ruth Ellis, the dentist's wife, resided in Warsash for several months, and became the last woman to be hanged in Britain. Photograph courtesy of Topfoto

Post Office, the policeman's house, the Newsagent and Butcher in Warsash Road

in a surgery in Warsash Road. She was a glamorous blonde, very smartly dressed, wearing a fur coat, high stiletto heels and red fingernails as she walked through the village on the rough roads. It was still a time of austerity in post-Second World War England, so no one failed to notice or talk about her. Ruth lived in Warsash for about five months. She left her husband and moved to London, where she met racing driver David Blakely with whom she had a relationship. He treated her harshly, causing her injuries. Ruth allegedly obtained a revolver, and was charged with the murder of Blakely by shooting him. She was found guilty and was sentenced to be hanged. In 1955 Ruth Ellis at the age of 28 years became the last woman to be hanged in Britain. Close by the Post Office, the police officer's house and the newsagent's home, faced with bricks and flint stones, made up a pleasant terrace. The shoe repairer Mr

Read worked in a small workshop behind the newsagent.

Stan Knapp ran a hairdressing shop for men, with a four-penny cut for boys, in a hut across the road. Mr Marshall established a fish and chip shop here circa 1940.

Vic Collins commenced a motor vehicle repair garage and dealership in a building close by in circa 1930. The building was used by the Home Guard during the Second World War, and by Jack Boardman, a used furniture dealer, after the war. Apartment homes are now situated on the site in 2006.

At the old Post Office, Dibles Road bears off on the right, until recently a through road to Fleet End. At this junction in circa 1940 three shops were located, Palmers the butcher, Everetts the chemist and St John's the baker, now the Warsash Nautical Bookshop. Further on a turning north off Dibles Road leads to Gravel Hill Cottages and Grays Terrace,

Victor Collins' first workshop in Warsash Road, Warsash

Victor Collins, motor cycle speedway champion

both marked on an 1870 map. In addition two old cottages, now converted into one dwelling, built circa 1750 stand in Dibles Bottom. It is a Grade 2 listed building, built partially of cob and wattle with a longstraw-thatched roof, named Willow Tree Cottage.

On the opposite side of the road stood a large machine used for grading and washing sand and gravel excavated from a quarry situated here. It was in use in circa 1930 until circa 1950, with the materials being carried away in the early period by steam lorries.

Large numbers of Stone Age Acheulean flint axe heads have been found in the Warsash and Hook quarries. This indicates early settlements with a manufacturing industry. Several axe heads are on display in the Fareham museum.

It is possible that flint axes were used to hollow ancient dugout canoes after first charring the wood. The remains of a canoe of this type, buried in mud alluvium, were discovered in 1888 at Botley, and stored there until 1913. Since then it has been kept in a Southampton museum, where hopefully it will receive dendrochronological testing to determine the date when it was constructed.

There is also natural sandstone to be found in Hampshire. Frank Bowman, now retired, who has been an excavator driver during his working life, has literally moved hundreds of these stones. He explained that these individual stones are always found under the top layer of gravel, and in the top of the underlying sand. They come in all sizes, often too large to move even with a machine. The outer surface is extremely hard and has on

occasions damaged an excavator's bucket. These stones are only ever found in a gravel and sand environment, giving belief that they have not been transported here by man or nature. The most famous stones were at Three Stone Bottom in Titchfield Common, by the A27 road, near where the MFI store now stands. The well-known legend told us that these three large stones crossed the road at midnight on New Year's Eve. During road works in recent years the stones were relocated and are now displayed, surrounded by grass, in West Street, Titchfield.

Further on in Dibles Road is a terrace of four cottages, named Ireland Cottages, built as homes for the nearby Ireland Farm workers.

Returning to Warsash Road, the first Congregational church was built on the northern side of the road in 1854, with a replacement being raised in 1889. The former church was then used as a church hall until its demolition in recent years. A manse of attractive appearance completed the group of buildings.

A short distance further is the red-brick Plymouth Brethren Church, built in 1904, named the Swinton Hall after the benefactor Caroline Swinton, who provided the land on which the church stands.

Opposite Swinton Hall stood Yew Tree Farm, although its earlier title on the 1870 map was Little Brook Farm. The farm house and buildings, together with several cottages, were demolished many years ago, and the barn was taken down in 2004. The Southdown Bus Company built an overnight garage here circa 1930. The bus drivers and conductors had to

The Post Office etc and Congregational Church

H E Palmer, the butcher in Warsash Road

rise very early, travel by bicycle from their homes to the garage, open up and get the bus engines warmed, and be at the Clock Tower for the first passengers at 5.30 am.

Close by a stream runs under the road in a pipe, which children crawled through on their way home from Sunday school, wearing their Sunday-best clothes.

In a wooden bungalow, halfway between the farm and Greenaway Lane, resided Mr Craig, who played the organ in St Mary's Church during the years circa 1930 to 1945, travelling there on a large bicycle, always at a sedate pace.

Greenaway Lane is passed, and on the left at the bend in the road stood Great Ireland Farm, as noted on an 1870 map. Across the road to the south stood Little Ireland Farm.

In 1900 Great Ireland Farm became Upper Brook Farm, and later it became a private house and a children's home named Horseshoe Lodge in circa 1960.

During the period approximately 1895 to 1915 a small brickyard was constructed with kilns to the north of Warsash Road on land owned by Mr Andrews, a farmer who lived in Upper Brook Farm. He employed Jack Rodgers from Poole as a supervisor. It was necessary in the course of the manufacture of a clamp brick to mix clay and cinders together before being fired. These cinders were obtained from Southampton Docks, where many ships were coal-burning. The cinders were transported to Warsash Hard in lighters and barges, and all available horses and carts were chartered to take the cinders to the brickyard.

To make maximum use of the transport the carts were first loaded with new bricks at the kilns, then taken to Warsash Hard, loaded into vessels and sent to destinations including the Isle of Wight, where they were used in the construction of Parkhurst Prison.

Several houses in Fleet End were also built with bricks from this yard.

Nurse Hill, the district midwife, during the years circa 1930 to circa 1943 resided in a bungalow near the Fleet End crossroads. She deserves special praise, with her round spread over a very wide area, on call at all hours, seven days a week, arriving on her bicycle in all weathers even during the Second World War. At that time virtually all children were born at home, with Nurse Hill in attendance for the delivery and aftercare. This remarkable lady lived to be over one hundred years of age.

The Warsash boundary is only a short distance further, close to the Locks Heath Junior School attended by many Fleet End and Warsash children. In 1924 a Gloster Grebe fighter aircraft which had been circling a friend's house ran into difficulties and crashed onto a wooden classroom, causing the death of one girl.

*A light aircraft crashed onto Locks Heath Junior School in Warsash Road in 1924,
causing the death of a girl from Fleet End*

*Locks Heath Junior School pupils and their teacher, Miss Banbury, in 1938.
Many of the pupils lived in Fleet End and Warsash*

Osborne Road, from Warsash Road to the Recreation Ground

Osborne and Pitchponds Roads were constructed in the late nineteenth century with very rough gravel surfaces, as all roads in the area were originally. They quickly became full of huge potholes filled with rainwater.

Pitchponds was a wild place of adventure, no houses at all until circa 1960, a high uncut hedge on one side, with a moor, trees and water on the southern side which was once part of the estuary.

The roads were not made up with a tarmac surface and pavements until 1965. Although Fareham Borough Council coordinated the work, and now undertake maintenance, much of the road improvements costs were paid by the frontagers. The amount that each house or landowner paid was determined by the length of their boundary adjoining the road.

This area had also been part of Titchfield Common. Eight detached and seven pairs of semi-detached cottages were built in Osborne Road from 1886 to 1900, also a terrace of four with flat roofs, all built in a line, close to the road.

James Lock, not being one to miss an opportunity, had four cottages built named Lock's Cottages. He also owned other houses in this road which are cement-rendered, probably using reclaimed materials from the chemical works.

Henry Woodford, while constructing the roof on Lock's Cottages, called out that he could see Osborne House on the Isle of Wight, hence Osborne Road was named.

The local authority built a number of houses in the 1930s, otherwise virtually all the land surrounding Osborne and Church Roads was under cultivation with strawberries. The growers that come to mind are Mr Ralph Moody, Mr Sandy, Mr Searle, Mr Hewett, Mr Coombs and the Jupe brothers. The work was very labour intensive, subject to crop failure due to frosts when the plant was in flower, insect problems or disease and the whims of the market, and to a crop that only produced for about eight weeks a year or so in May, June and July according to the weather. The soil in the fields was full of stones in which the strawberry plants seemed to thrive.

In order to keep the fruit clean from soil during the growing stage straw was carefully laid under the flowers and leaves, where the fruit would nestle as it ripened.

With a need to protect the flowering plants from frost, and to produce an earlier crop which would achieve a higher price at market, particularly in London, glass cloches were introduced. There was the initial outlay, of course, so not all could afford the cost or the extra work and time involved with removing the cloches for ventilation and irrigation, and replacing in the evenings.

During the spring and summer most housewives worked in the fields; the schools closed for three weeks' holiday so that the children could also help.

Strawberry growing was a very precarious occupation, causing the Parish magazine to write an article in 1914 regarding the situation. "The prices being paid for strawberries were very low, as the fruits were so abundant that year, leading to serious doubt whether strawberry growing was likely to become a permanent industry in the district."

The strawberries were cultivated in a three-year cycle system. Young plants were planted in the autumn in one third of the field and would fruit during the following summer with a limited yield. The second year plants would crop well, as would the third year plants. It was considered prudent to dig out the third year plants and continue the cycle. Young plants were obtained by the layering system. After fruiting the plants would send out long shoots, which formed into plants with roots. These were held firm in the soil by means of a large stone being placed on the new shoot. By the autumn the new plants were large enough to be removed, the young shoot would be cut from the mother plant and

transplanting took place. Generally second year plants were selected for the regeneration process.

A large proportion of villagers grew strawberries in their gardens as a sideline to supplement their income.

In the years 1920–1960 Mr Cecil Sandy ran a coal business from the yard adjacent to his home in Osborne Road. The business had evolved from his father's days in circa 1880 when coal was delivered by sea and stored in a yard behind The Rising Sun.

The coal cart was horse-drawn, until a Clayton steam lorry was purchased circa 1920, its water tanks being replenished daily from Pitch Pond. In circa 1930 the steam lorry was replaced by a Ford lorry, with Mr Sandy also obtaining supplies of coal from the goods yard at Swanwick Railway Station.

Mrs Wills also resided in Osborne Road for many years, with a lovely appearance which dated back to a much

Mr C Sandy's steam coal lorry

Warsash Football Club Senior XI 1949-1950
(front row left to right) A Leach, R Packman, P Coombs, A Buckett and C Jupe
(rear row) T Cozens, A Foy, Ron Buckett, P Burnett, J Worley, K Edwards, R Buckett, R Swain

earlier time. Even in 1944, she always wore a three-quarter length black dress with black stockings and shoes, her hair made into a bun, with a snow-white starched apron that was changed each afternoon after she had done her morning's housework and food preparation.

Jim, her husband, had been the skipper of the crab and lobster boat Gem.

In 1915 Ethel Gee was born and resided in Osborne Road, later becoming friendly with an ex-Royal Navy man, Harry Houghton, who also lived in Warsash. They both obtained employment at the Government Underwater Detection Establishment at Portland in Dorset, with Miss Gee working as a filing clerk in the drawing office with a high risk security clearance.

In 1961 they were both arrested, charged and convicted of passing secret information to the Soviet spies Gordon Lonsdale and his communication team Helen and Peter Kroger. The punishment for Houghton and Gee was a term of fifteen years in jail.

The recreation ground that was inaugurated in 1911 is also situated in Osborne Road, with the pavilion paid for by public subscription.

The football team was officially known as the Warsash Crabs, but not in a derogatory manner, and had many successes over the years.

In 1920 a large ex-army field gun, but not in working condition, was placed in one corner of the ground. It became very popular with children clambering on it, although it was taken away and recycled in the Second World War. The grass tennis courts were installed in 1952.

Opposite the recreation ground resided the former Warsash schoolmaster Mr Threlfall, with his wife bequeathing their

Warsash brass band in 1922

Skipper Arthur Jupe with the remains of his yacht's mast after being hit by the wing of a seaplane in flight in 1935

home to the church to be used as a replacement for the older vicarage.

There was one other house nearby, with a sweetshop owned by Mrs Searle. During 1945 a large area of moorland was still in evidence next to and behind these two properties.

In 1935 Mr Arthur Jupe Snr and fifteen-year-old Harry Pannell, both residents of Osborne Road, were about to take part in a yacht race at Cowes. They were sailing a six-metre yacht named Dragon and were in collision with a sailing whaler. Requiring repairs, the yacht proceeded to return to Warsash. At a position midway between Calshot and the Hamble River, an RAF flying

boat taking off came up from astern at high speed.

The aircraft had left the water when her wing struck the yacht's mast about four metres above the boom. The broken mast went overboard with sails and rigging in the water. Arthur, at the helm, was carried several metres along the deck, and received cuts and injuries to the neck and shoulders by the falling mast and rigging. The pilot skilfully brought the aircraft down, narrowly missing the yacht, and taxied to Calshot.

Harry was in the cabin and escaped injury, but he had a good story to tell seventy years later. The yacht was towed to a jetty by an RAF motor vessel.

Church Road, from the Victory Hall to St Mary's Church

This road was built as a driveway to the mansion named Hook House, with a gate and gatekeeper's lodge at the southern end, in circa 1790, close to the site where the church was to be built later. An additional gate and gatekeeper's lodge were added at the northern end in 1871.

The driveway appears on an 1870 map clearly showing that it was planted with an avenue of trees on both sides of its half-mile length. This would have been spectacular had it survived, similar to the long avenues which one sees in France. The dry soil of this area, with the solid gravel subsoil, was not suitable for the trees and most of them died.

The lovely church of St Mary's, in the new parish of Hook with Warsash, with a combined population of about 1,200, was designed by Raphael Brandon, with the vicarage, school and schoolmaster's house being built at the same time in 1871, and endowed by Mr Arthur

St Mary's Church, Hook with Warsash (Author)

Hornby of Hook House. It all sounds very attractive, but this was a remote and lonely area, surrounded by moor, gorse and heather, with a walk of over half a mile on a stony road to the small hamlet of Warsash. It is not surprising that headmasters and their wives at the school tended to move on after a short time.

The electric organ installed in the church was purchased from Warsash House prior to its demolition in 1937. Joan Collins recalls visiting the mansion with the vicar to arrange the purchase.

There were four pairs of semi-detached houses constructed circa 1910 on the west side of the road, and a pair on the left further down. Most of the land was under cultivation with strawberries, although some moor with gorse and heather remained.

The fields were owned by Mr Ernest Moody, the Jupe brothers, Mr Cozens and Mr W Mitchell, Mr W Johns, Mr E Buckett, Mr Harding, Mr H Rowe and Mr T Boyes.

A short distance further, near the church, a lane turns in to the left. A small corrugated iron church hall stood here on land where the new vicarage has been built. The land beyond, which is now Sea Scout accommodation and a boys' football ground, was moor with gorse and heather in circa 1960.

The first vicarage, built of stone, situated to the north of the present church hall, matched the architecture of the school and the schoolmaster's house.

During the Second World War the stained glass windows in the church were damaged by a V1 bomb. The east windows were replaced with stained glass in 1950, but the west windows were replaced with clear glass only. A gateway once existed in the southern boundary wall, wide enough for a horse and carriage to pass through. It has been closed with matching stone and is partially overgrown, although the gate hinge pins are still visible embedded in the wall. Was this the private entrance for the Hornbys from Hook, when alighting from their carriage at the church door?

The small gate in the northern wall led to the vicarage, and was used by the vicar.

An interesting paragraph in the parish magazine in 1903 comments that the lychgate is a stopping place for the bodies of departed Christians, and a resting place for those who have travelled far to get to the church. It is not to be used as a sauntering place for idle boys, smoking is forbidden, and persons are not allowed to stroll around the churchyard while services are taking place.

The Church of England school, standing opposite the church, opened in 1872. Two extra brick classrooms were built later. There were two large cast iron coke-burning stoves for heating the large schoolroom, which took hours to warm up, with the boys being coke monitors.

The toilets were in a separate building at the rear of the school and built at the same time, not the flush modern type, but where buckets were in use. Former pupils will be pleased to know that the toilet block is now a listed building!

Hook with Warsash School circa 1910

Mr Harradon, headmaster at Hook with Warsash School

Moor Hill, from St Mary's Church to Hook Park

Immediately past the church stood the entrance gates and a single-storey lodge, erected in circa 1788.

Mr and Mrs Windsor were the gatekeepers from 1903 to at least 1914, with Mr and Mrs Jim Cripps living here from about 1938 until 1950.

This was the only entrance to Hook House with a horse and carriage from the Warsash side of the Hook estuary. This driveway, named Moor Hill, was set in a lovely rhododendron wood, with an ornamental bridge over a stream, as mentioned earlier. There were masses of golden kingcups in blossom in the spring, with the road rising to the cluster of houses in Hook, passing an ever-running spring where boys and girls would stop for a drink.

At the brow of the hill, on the right, stood a black wooden barn surrounded by primrose plants, making a pretty sight, with the estate dairy and three cottages on the left completing the picture. The dairy and cottages were demolished many years ago.

Moor Hill now arrives at the junction with Hook Park Road, where at a little distance on the right can be seen Pink Cottage, formerly the laundry for the Hornby estate.

It should be noted that Moor Hill, which is now only a footpath and bridleway, was in 1970 wide enough to allow two cars to pass each other in places. Two well-used footpaths were situated close to the lodge; one went to the Maritime Academy in Newtown Road, the other to Fleet End Bottom.

The General Stores in Fleet End Road

Fleet End Road, from Warsash Road to Hook Village

All the area which is now Fleet End was part of Titchfield Common until 1864.

Within a short time James Lock, the entrepreneur, built The Jolly Farmer public house and a terrace of cottages nearby named Fleet End Terrace. The cottages are named on an 1870 map, so one can assume that they were constructed at least two or three years before that date.

During the strawberry season each year travellers and gypsies in caravans camped in the Jolly Field opposite the public house, as they did in many other fields in the area while picking fruit. Their tents or benders consisted of wooden poles bent into a semicircle with the ends pushed into the soil, and covered with waterproof sheeting.

At the crossroads with Dibles Road, a road with a gravel surface called New Road crosses an area now named Warsash

Common, leading to St Mary's Church. Further on Fleet End Road dips into a banked valley, probably at one time the inner shore of the Hook Estuary. An 1837 tithe map shows several cottages in the valley, possibly built by squatters on the common.

Daisy Crockford circa 1909, later to become Daisy Kieser, employed at Warsash House in later years

Hook Village, Hook Park Road and Chilling Lane

Mrs Jeffrey, Mrs Silvester, Mrs Bartholomew, Mrs Gregory and families

When arriving at the crossroads at Hook Village a very interesting cluster of buildings is found, which formed part of the Hornby Estate.

To the east stands a terrace named Hook Cottages, with lozenge window glazing, built in 1846. The tenants in 1908 were Messrs Silvester, Bartholomew, Gregory and Jeffery and their families. Close by is the former blacksmith's house, workshop and forge, run by the Silvester family for several generations.

To the west can be seen the former carpenter's and wheelwright's house and workshop, built at the same time. During the early 1900s Mr Newbury bought the premises, now the Nook and Cranny restaurant.

Wagons were produced, and joinery products made for installation in many houses built in the area. There was also a large sawmill and a crane at the rear of this property, where complete tree trunks were sawn by mechanical means into timber suitable for house construction and joinery.

Further on in Hook Park Road stood a pair of thatched cottages, now made into one dwelling, and the gamekeeper's cottage in the woods. A Post Office letterbox was set in the estate supervisor's thatched cottage residence further on, with three collections daily. Situated

The wheelwright's and wagon builder's workshop in Hook Village circa 1920, now the Nook and Cranny restaurant

NEWBURY'S HOOK SAW
MILL ABOUT 1920.
THE BIG CROSS-CUT SAW
IS IN OPERATION AND THE
LITTLE GIANT HARD AT
WORK. "CJ" (WITH BIKE) IS
DIRECTING FRANK BOWMAN
WHILE TOM HARDING CLIMBS
ONTO HIS DRIVING SEAT.
YOUNG WYN NEWBURY
TAKES IN THE SCENE.

Newbury's large saw in Hook Village at the rear of the wagon building workshop circa 1920
Drawing courtesy of Mr Frank Claxton

Newbury's cart being used to transport strawberries to Swanwick Railway Station

in a lane on the left, a little distance on, was a terrace of four cottages, now converted to a pair named Hook Farm Cottages.

Continuing a short distance, on the right is the former site of a terrace of cottages and a dairy. Nearby the two Hook House carriageways converged, straight on for Hook House or turn right for the church and Warsash.

Returning to Hook Village, take the road to Chilling and Solent Breezes. The attractive Fish House stands on the right, built circa 1850.

It was considered a superior residence, suitable for a gentleman's occupation, with a tennis lawn and fine views over The Solent. One hundred and forty acres of land were also included, with numerous stables, a chaise house and farm buildings. In later years the house and farm buildings were divided, with the stables

and farm buildings forming the present Solent Court.

Across the road from Fish House a narrow lane led to another estate property, Green Lane Farm, a holding of forty acres of arable land, with a pair of brick-built cottages, a barn and stabling.

Further on in Chilling Lane was a terrace of three cottages with gardens, named Mosels. There were also large arable fields, with Mr Burge renting 43 acres, and Mr Gibbings renting a further 123 acres. The cottages were sold in 1911 with a right granted that the purchaser could take water from the Brownwich Pond. Mosels cottages were demolished in circa 1960.

Continuing in Chilling Lane, the Little Chilling Farm cottage, formerly a pair of cottages, is situated some way back from the road. At the time of the 1911 sale there were 147 acres of arable land and twenty acres of woodland. Thatched stabling for three horses was available, with three cow pens.

A short distance on in Chilling Lane, with views over the sea, stood Great Chilling, a fine half-timbered Elizabethan stock farm dating from circa 1550, and inhabited until 1950.

Mr Horace Mortimer purchased this picturesque building as a pair of cottages from the Hook House Estate in 1911. Mr Burge was the occupying tenant of the farm at that time.

There was a panelled hall with quaintly carved figures on the door jambs, and one panelled wall in one of the sitting rooms.

Work was undertaken to convert the cottages into one dwelling, with Tudor style fireplaces, moulded ceilings and an oak-beamed staircase added. Great Chilling was a beautiful place with a garden and orchard, and in a nearby wood primroses and bluebells blossomed in the spring.

Mrs Russell, an American, resided here during the First World War, and entertained American troops stationed in the district.

Mr and Mrs Dibben, the well known Southampton builders merchants, lived here from 1939 to 1945, with Mrs Dibben inviting Mr and Mrs Fuller and their three sons to live with her in this large house while her husband was away during the war.

Gertrude Lawrence, the famous actress, visited the house during the Second World War, with young George

Little Chilling Farm in Chilling Lane (Author)

Fuller presenting her with a bouquet of flowers. Lt Col David Niven, the renowned British actor, serving with an army commando unit, was also a visitor at a later date.

The farm originally consisted of 142 acres of arable land and pasture, with all the buildings associated with this type of farm.

It was considered at the 1911 sale that there were great opportunities for building development speculators, who may be interested in this site with its sea views.

The farmhouse was purchased in 1946 by Mr Jenkyns, who later sold it to an oil company. The Council for the Preservation of Rural England encouraged its restoration, but it stood empty for several years, and eventually the condition of the building deteriorated and it was demolished.

Great Chilling circa 1550 to circa 1950

Warsash at War, 1939 to 1945

Before the commencement of the Second World War Warsash had been a very quiet village, most of the area being cultivated with strawberries and other soft fruit. Many of the holdings were about four to five acres in size, each one run by one man and his wife or occasionally by families. Local wives and itinerant travellers were employed during the summer, and children during the school holidays.

The population was small in number, so most of the villagers knew one another, or at least the families. Many men not employed in horticulture worked in the boatyards at Hamble and Swanwick, or in the Hamble aircraft factories. A large number were skippers, or members of the crew, in yachts and fishing boats, or served in the Royal Navy, Royal Marines and the Merchant Navy, particularly in the large liners running from Southampton. The construction and transport industries also employed a smaller number.

The first outward sign of war was the setting up of an air raid warden base in the original Victory Hall, with sandbags being filled for the protection of the

The hand powered siren from the Victory Hall, used during power failures when the electric siren would be out of action (Author)

Air Raid Wardens wearing steel helmets, with respirators tied to their chests which would be used in the event of a gas attack

A Bofors anti-aircraft gun still exists at Hamble, similar to the guns positioned near the ferry at Warsash and at Hook Point

building. An air raid siren was erected on a steel pole, and when used could be heard across the village. A portable siren was used in the event of an electricity failure, operated manually by turning a handle.

A brick pillbox approximately fifteen feet square and seven feet high was erected in the centre of the Clock Tower crossroads. There were small apertures on all four sides so that machine guns or rifles could be used in the event of an invasion.

Concrete anti-aircraft gun emplacements were built on the foreshore near the ferry and at Hook Point and are still intact.

A brick air raid shelter was erected near The Rising Sun, and metal shelters in the school playground. A mock bungalow built on the cliff top at Chilling housed

two 12-pounder quick-firing Hotchkiss guns. Shells could be fired at fifteen rounds a minute at any German motor torpedo boat or destroyer that may have made incursions into The Solent and Southampton Water. Imitation windows and doors that could be opened easily concealed the guns. The guns were manufactured before 1903, and had been previously installed at Fort Blockhouse, the submarine base in Gosport.

They were returned after the war, and are now used as saluting guns by the Royal Navy at the entrance to Portsmouth harbour. The guns are fired when foreign Heads of State on board ships are visiting Britain, to celebrate the Queen's birthday, and on Remembrance Day in November each year.

Four concrete and brick structures were built into the cliff face at Chilling and

One of the two Hotchkiss guns in position at Chilling during WW2, now returned to Fort Blockhouse in Gosport, at the entrance to Portsmouth Harbour, and fired as saluting guns on important occasions. The guns were mounted in a different manner during the war

Three searchlight embrasures in the cliff face at Chilling; the windows were fitted after the war. The two 12-pound Hotchkiss guns were hidden in the Bungalow Battery on the cliff top, seen on the right-hand side of the picture

The searchlight embrasure at Brownwich,
photo taken in 2005

An observation post, still in existence, stands on the cliff above the one remaining searchlight embrasure at Brownwich.

There were other buildings containing generators to power the searchlights, and living accommodation for the artillerymen. Still in existence, one hundred metres inland, is a control building. It was part of a bombing range used by Fleet Air Arm personnel when training Barracuda aircraft pilots flying from the airfield at Lee-on-the-Solent.

Brownwich housing searchlights, with their beams sweeping across the water, and operating in conjunction with the guns at Chilling and those on Calshot Castle.

Many local men were required to serve in the armed services, in all the theatres of war throughout the world. Some were captured by the enemy and kept in prisoner-of-war camps in Germany for up to five years; others were in Italy or the Far East.

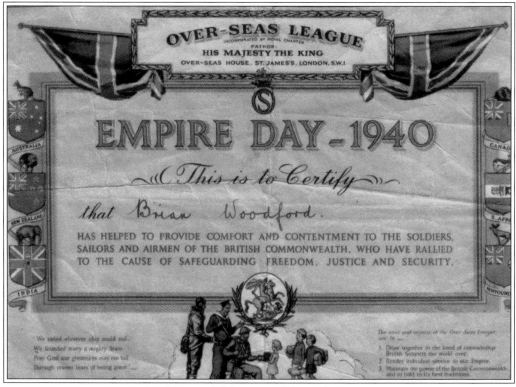

A certificate awarded to most children during the war

Members of the Auxiliary Fire Service under instruction in Warsash

Householders were given corrugated steel Anderson air raid shelters for use in their homes. Pits were dug in the gardens, approximately two metres in length and depth and 1.5 metres wide. The shelter components were placed in the pit, bolted together, and then lined with concrete to prevent ingress of water. Filled sandbags were placed around the entrance to prevent blast damage, and the whole shelter covered with soil and grass to avoid detection from the air.

They were cold and damp, but sleeping in them was better than being indoors when bombers were overhead. Some people used Morrison shelters indoors; they were similar to a steel household table with people sheltering underneath. Mr Fuger, who ran the bus company before the war, became concerned when his Anderson shelter, promised several

times, had not arrived. He dug a large pit in the garden and buried one of his buses.

The cellar in The Salterns, now Admirals House, in Newtown Road, was also regularly used as a shelter during the periods of German bombing.

Early in the war gas masks were issued to the civilian population and were carried everywhere, including to school. Adhesive tape was placed on windows to form small squares, hopefully to lessen the deadly effect of flying glass during bombing raids. Black curtains and blinds were fastened to all windows and doors to hide any light. German aircraft many miles away could see a single light that may be showing. The wrath of the air raid warden was severe, that is if the Germans did not bomb you first.

One of the earlier properties in the district to be damaged by bombing was

Jesmond in Locks Road. Mrs Peggy Scott, the St Mary's vicar's wife, was staying there at the time, shortly after giving birth to Peter, her third child, but they were not injured.

The first house to suffer bomb damage in Warsash was the home of Mr Alfred Claxton in Warsash Road, Fleet End. A bomb dropped in the garden approximately three metres from the front room of the house, where four members of the family were sitting. There was extensive damage with everyone being blown across the room, hit by bricks and buried by timber and rubble. They all miraculously survived without serious injury or cuts from flying glass.

Many other bombs were dropped causing blast damage and broken windows. Several unexploded bombs lay in land where Burgundy Close now stands, with several residents being evacuated until the bomb disposal squad had rendered the bombs safe and removed them.

One afternoon during the break at Hook School a German fighter aircraft flew in very low from over the churchyard and fired its machine guns. Most of the children were in the playground, therefore it was incredible that none of the children was killed or injured.

The Local Defence Volunteers, dressed in civilian clothes and wearing LDV armbands, had their headquarters in a building in Warsash Road. Eventually they were provided with army uniforms and renamed the Home Guard. They were in normal day employment, plus

A Home Guard shoulder flash,
worn on the upper arm of the uniform

A Platoon of the Warsash Home Guard marching in Church Road after attending a church service

The special Home Guard unit, with a secret underground base at Hook, who would have become saboteurs, capable of infiltrating enemy supply and communication lines after an invasion with the dairy and dairy cottages in the background

overtime work, and were required to attend training drills with the Home Guard in the evenings, weekends and some duties overnight. Corporal Ted Woodford kept his rifle at home ready for use, as did all the Home Guard. On the night of 10th April 1941 he saw parachutes descending, and ran to the shore with his rifle. He heard shouting from six survivors of a Royal Navy vessel which had been blown up by a mine in Southampton Water. Sergeant Tom Cozens, who was also the harbour master, living in Greenaway Lane, also heard the shouting. He quickly went to the shore, where he and Ted rowed a small boat to the harbour master's launch moored in the river.

They went to the rescue, picking up three men who had been in the water for forty-five minutes, while a Royal Navy vessel rescued the others. Ted and Tom were mentioned in a Home Guard report.

The parachutes which were seen had acoustic mines attached and would lie on the seabed, being triggered by the sound of a ship or a boat's propeller beating on the water. The report on the incident concluded, "I consider that the very prompt action of these men of the Home Guard is worthy of the highest praise."

Another civilian group formed in the village in 1940, recruited from the Home Guard, and top secret was the No 5 special patrol of No 6 Group of the 203 Reserve.

They were trained in guerrilla warfare at Coleshill House, near Swindon, using explosives and equipment not available to the main Home Guard units. Their task was to lie low, and to emerge after an invasion. Known as the suicide squad with a life expectancy of a few weeks, they became fully-armed saboteurs, capable of infiltrating enemy supply and communication lines.

An underground hideout was built in Hook near the gamekeeper's cottage, with sleeping quarters, stores for food, weapons, ammunition and explosives, all very clandestine, with a concealed entrance and an escape tunnel. An observation post was also constructed in the wood near Pink Cottage.

Prior to the completion of their hideout they stored a very large amount of explosives and ammunition in a shed in the allotments, and in an outhouse in Newtown Road.

Persons serving in this group were Bill Swatheridge, Bill Foy, Ron Browning, Peter Fuller, Sergeant Joe Bowell from Hamble, Corporal Jim Street and George Hill.

Several villagers joined the Auxiliary Fire Service as fire-fighters at Warsash and in fire stations in neighbouring villages.

In July 1940 a Royal Navy shore establishment named HMS Tormentor was commissioned in Newtown Road, using the buildings built for the Royal Naval Air Service in 1913, now the Warsash Maritime Academy.

The small yacht maintenance facility named Stone Pier Yard, situated by the Lobster Quay, was taken over by the Royal Navy, who greatly extended the yard. A slipway was built and hauling-up equipment installed, so that vessels could be repaired out of the water. Workshops and storerooms were built for the engineering, electrical, ordnance, shipwright, blacksmith, rigging and painting departments. Fuel tanks were buried underground where the northern car park is now situated, and a refuelling jetty installed at the yard.

There was eventually, in 1944, a complement of 2,400 officers and ratings working in the base at the repair yard, and as crews in the patrol and assault craft. In addition, there were 443 Wren officers and Wrens undertaking jobs previously done by men, including manning boats as coxswains, engineers and deckhands. They carried men and supplies to vessels moored in the Hamble River, at Southampton and in The Solent. Towing and mooring vessels were other tasks, working all hours in all weathers.

Frederick Loader, Master at Arms at HMS Tormentor, July 1943 to November 1945 attending a ceremonial parade with traditional frock coat, sword and medals

Wrens dismantling a marine engine in the Royal Navy workshops in Stone Pier Yard in 1943
Photograph courtesy of the Imperial War Museum London, negative number A19498

Wrens were also employed in the yard, manufacturing bow and stern ropes and fenders; others were working in the engineering and gunnery workshops and stores. Some of the girls had undertaken courses at Slough in carpentry, welding and painting and were working with the shipwrights. The remainder were employed in the base in Newtown Road as drivers, telephone operators, cooks, stewards, administrators, writers, communicators, nurses and stores assistants. Many local girls serving with the Wrens at Tormentor were welcomed by the Admiralty as they were living at home and did not require accommodation. Amongst these were Nancy and Lucy Berryman, Mona Peckham, Iris Kettle, Marjorie Bucket,

Stella and Wendy Packman, Doris Brown, Betty and Kathleen Cox, Anne Jupe, Eileen Lewis and Peggy Skinner.

Patricia Mountbatten, now Rt Hon the Countess Mountbatten, served as a seventeen-year-old Wren in the communications office, commencing in 1943 for a period of fifteen months. Her quarters were with other Wrens in Hook Bye, now named Christmas House, in Hook Park. Her father, Admiral Lord Louis Mountbatten, visited the base and repair yard on several occasions. In January 1942 Lord Louis issued a general invitation for designs to be submitted for a Combined Operations badge. Many drawings were submitted, with the final choice being the work of Lt D A Grant of HMS Tormentor. His design represented the three services, consisting of a naval crown, a fouled anchor, a tommy gun and an eagle.

The badge of the Combined Operations personnel, designed by an officer in HMS Tormentor at Warsash. Photograph courtesy of Mr Hubert Long of the Military Heraldry Society

As the base and facilities expanded, additional sleeping accommodation was required, therefore men were billeted with Warsash householders. Naval ratings working in the harbour boom defence system and persons who had been bombed out of their homes in Southampton and Portsmouth also found accommodation in the village.

The Admiralty requisitioned all the large houses and several smaller ones. These included Golf House, Dormy House, Sunburst, Creek House, Hook Bye and Bridge House in Hook Park, Red Tiles, The Salterns, Rodneys, Tideways, Springfields and Hamble Bank in Newtown Road. The Salterns was equipped and used as HMS Tormentor's medical quarters, or in naval terminology the sick bay. Warsash Court, Stone Cottage and Pond Cottage were included with several others in Shore Road. The Rising Sun Hotel accommodated stokers,

with the bars remaining open to the public. Shore House became the quarters for the engineering officers, including Alec Rose, who was appointed as a sub-lieutenant to HMS Tormentor in 1944 for six months.

To provide further accommodation metal Nissan huts were erected close to Shore House.

HMS Tormentor's first role was to train boat crews and men of the Vth Army Corps and the 5th and 12th Commando units to undertake raids of short duration on the European coast in 1941. This involved a small number of troops for reconnaissance purposes, sabotage, or to bring back important pieces of German equipment, eg radar, which could be analysed by our scientists.

German prisoners were also brought back, no doubt to obtain information.

Vessels from Warsash took part in many other operations, with Tormentor becoming a very important Combined Operations base. The commandos were selected as men with exceptional physical ability, determination and endurance, and were drawn from most army regiments.

The Dieppe Raid (Operation Jubilee) took place in 1942 with 2,000 troops embarking at Shoreham in seventy-eight of HMS Tormentor's Landing Craft Personnel, Large (LCPLs). These vessels, originally called R raiding boats, were 37 feet in length, built of seven-layer plywood, and carried 25 men and their equipment. They had been constructed by Higgins, boat builders in New Orleans in 1940 and 1941. Each vessel was powered by a 250hp Hall-Scott engine with a speed of 20 knots, and was capable of jumping over a bar or log.

An excellent book *HMS Tormentor 1940-1946 A Brief History* by Lt Cdr Kenneth Scott RNVR, who served in HMS Tormentor, is well worth reading. It relates in detail the many raids carried out by the Warsash-based vessels. It is not so brief with 240 pages.

A Royal Navy motor boat base named Greenways operated from the Universal Shipyard in Sarisbury. Several top secret miniature submarines named X Craft were assembled there, carrying out trials in The Solent, each with a crew of four men.

Heavy bombing of Southampton and Portsmouth commenced in 1940, with night and daylight raids.

On one occasion a very large number of German bombers flew over Southampton Water in daylight on their way to Southampton. The RAF were unable to engage the enemy before they had dropped their bombs, but a battle was fought later over Calshot.

RAF personnel were constantly travelling in their vehicles to and from Newtown Road. They disembarked near the Tormentor pier, on their way to the RAF base at Calshot, where the Short Sunderland and Catalina flying boats were maintained, both types of aircraft being very important in anti-submarine warfare.

In 1941 several Free French motor gunboats arrived and moored in the river. General de Gaulle's son Phillipe was a member of one of the boat's crew, and was accommodated in Tormentor.

Lt Cdr Douglas Fairbanks Jnr KBE, DSC, US Navy Reserve, the well-known film star, came to Warsash, serving in a small raiding vessel in one of Tormentor's flotillas during 1942 to gain experience.

The Duke of Edinburgh, as Prince Philip of Greece, serving in the Royal Navy as a lieutenant, visited Tormentor to visit his cousin Wren Patricia Mountbatten.

One of the seventy-eight Landing Craft Personnel, or R Boats, based at HMS Tormentor and used in the landings at Dieppe, also on D-Day and at Walcheren in Holland. Photograph courtesy of Lt Colin Kitching RNVR Rtd

Red Tiles in Newtown Road, built in 1935 for the former Secretary of State for Foreign Affairs,
Sir Austen Chamberlain, and leased to the famous actor Lt Cdr Ralph Richardson RNVR in circa 1941
whilst he was serving as a pilot in the Fleet Air Arm

The famous actor and actress, Sir Laurence Olivier and Vivienne Leigh, who starred in many films, lived in Hook Park while Sir Laurence was serving in the Fleet Air Arm.

Ralph Richardson, residing in Red Tiles in Newtown Road, also served with the Fleet Air Arm as a pilot at HMS Raven, the air station at Eastleigh, travelling there by motor cycle.

He owned a ferocious dog who lay in wait for any schoolboy who dared to pass Red Tiles. Ralph on one such occasion paid up half-a-crown to replace a pair of the author's torn trousers!

In August 1942 two British light aircraft collided, a Tiger Moth and a Fairey Swordfish, both crashing in Brook Lane, one in a field adjacent to the junction with Greenaway Lane.

While constructing a rifle range in Hook Park soldiers discovered the overgrown ice house of the former Hook House.

A wooden jetty was constructed by Canadian army engineers opposite The Rising Sun. They also built the jetties by the lobster pond, running parallel to the shore, which were used before D-Day, when commandos embarked for Normandy. Moorings were laid the length of the river to take the forthcoming armada.

Many strawberry growers and women were directed to work in factories and boatyards, with most of the fields being turned over to food production, and the grassland in Hook Park ploughed to grow wheat.

Due to the shortage of labour strawberry growers would occasionally go to the senior school and ask if children could help to pick the fruit in school time. There was always a ready show of hands, as the volunteers would be paid, and a cooperative headmaster.

The school holidays in the summer were divided into two parts, with three weeks during the strawberry season and two weeks later. Children were then able to help at harvest time to build the wheat stooks in the fields, and to pick up the potatoes in the fields. They were paid, but there was nothing to spend the money on, so it went into their Post Office saving books.

The Government was always encouraging everyone to save with 'Buy a Spitfire or a Ship Week'. A large progress of savings board would be erected in Fareham West Street. Children felt that they were also helping with the war effort.

Hook School had a vegetable garden in the field where the church hall now stands, with pupils working there during school time for two or three hours a week. They also tended the crops in their fathers' gardens and allotments at weekends.

There were three teachers at the school during the war. Miss Terry taught the five-year-old children; those of six and seven years were with Mrs Graham, who later became the headmistress. The very pleasant headmaster, Mr Harradon, who had joined the school in 1920 and taught for twenty-seven years, tutored the remainder of children up to eleven years of age.

Most families kept chickens for eggs and rabbits for the table, with several people who owned a field keeping pigs. The government kept a good watch, and made a regulation that if a person reared two pigs then they could slaughter one for themselves, but the second one went to the Ministry of Food.

Ration books were issued to the entire population which limited the amount of food that families could buy. There was only a very small amount of food available, and no luxuries such as oranges, bananas, peaches, crisps, orange squash, ice cream, coffee or wine, and only a few occasional sweets, chocolates or plain biscuits. As most people had gardens or allotments there were usually plenty of vegetables.

Clothes were also rationed, and difficult to find, as the shops in the towns had been destroyed by the German bombing.

Children were encouraged to write to children in the USA, no doubt to help foster Anglo-American relations, with several still corresponding today.

People sometimes became reluctant to go to a shelter during air raids, as it may be several hours or more before the all-clear siren was sounded, with perhaps no raiders appearing at all. An additional system was introduced so that production in factories could continue uninterrupted. This had a four-minute warning, and a special siren at Hamble or Fawley with a distinctive noise. When this occurred you can imagine the speed with which people dived for shelter.

All the steel railings outside houses, parks, fields and the school were removed to be recycled for the war effort. Collections were made for aluminium saucepans and books for the same reason.

Village life in many ways went on as before. There was a very active Girl Guides group, the 1st Warsash, with Mona Peckham being the very able

The Warsash Guides camp in Bramdean in 1945

Guide Mistress, also serving in the Wrens at that time. The Guides were dancing around the maypole in the vicarage garden when the ribbons became entwined. The vicar was asked to obtain a ladder and climb to the top of the pole to resolve the problem! On another occasion he was playing the piano on the stage in the Victory Hall, with the Guides swinging their arms to give the effect of angry trees. The Guides had an attack of the giggles which annoyed the vicar causing him to play faster!

The faster and harder he played the more the girls giggled, until the piano moved over the stage on its castors, bringing the house down with laughter. It was no surprise that the vicar would not allow girls in the church choir. The Guides also underwent tests in the vicarage to obtain their childcare and cookery badges and attended a camp for one week, sleeping in tents at a farm at Bramdean.

There were generally about five boys in the St Mary's Church choir. They were expected to attend Matins and Evensong services, listen to two sermons each Sunday and attend choir practice one evening a week. A small annual payment was made with deductions for any absence. Worse still, the choirboy's parents would receive a visit from the vicar during the following week to report the serious misdemeanour, always at teatime, of course! The boys attended the children's service on Sundays and, when confirmed, the 8.00 am Communion. Eventually they rebelled and negotiated an arrangement with the vicar. The boys were allowed to read a book in the choir stalls during the Matins sermon, and could leave the church before the evening sermon. On their first evening of freedom they celebrated by having a swig of the Communion wine which was kept in the vestry. The Reverend Scott was a very pleasant and enthusiastic vicar during the years 1941 to 1947, later becoming a bishop in South Africa.

Several boys joined the Scout group at Park Gate, with the leader Mr Everett the chemist, aided by his wife, using their home for meetings. Camp and field craft exercises were undertaken in Winnard's Estate at Sarisbury, which at that time was very overgrown. Mr Everett later purchased the large woodlands in Titchfield Lane, Fontley, and donated it to the Hampshire Scout Association for the benefit of all Scouts.

Most children attended Sarisbury Senior School, now Brookfield, for secondary education at eleven years of age. The school catchment area included the surrounding villages with the addition of Titchfield. All the pupils were accommodated in the small seven-classroom original school, with a quadrangle in the centre.

The school leaving age was fourteen years. The headmaster at Sarisbury, Mr Skilton, who lived in Warsash, ruled with a thin cane kept in his office and the fear of the consequences, which worked very well.

Most pupils did not get the cane and respected the headmaster. He had a rule that any boy passing him in the road would salute as a mark of courtesy, and he would return the salute, even when riding his bicycle.

Mr Skilton also took steps to encourage tidiness and public responsibility by placing an object such as a book or a magazine on the floor of a passageway. He would then hide out of sight; woe betide a pupil who failed to pick it up. On one occasion two boys played truant for one lesson. They were detected and questioned by Mr Skilton, the reason for absence being that they did not like country dancing. He gave them an alternative, and allowed them to work in the school vegetable garden. What good fortune!

There were two cinemas at Fareham which children and villagers frequented

St Mary's Church choir circa 1944

if they had time, travelling there by bus. Southampton and Portsmouth were rarely visited, as these towns had been reduced to piles of brick rubble by German bombing, with hundreds of people killed and thousands injured in each city. There was always the possibility of further raids.

Enjoyable Christmas parties were provided for the local children by HMS Tormentor, with huge trifles and cakes and a present. Where did they get those from?

Children received few presents at Christmas, perhaps a second-hand bicycle or a book, which were treasured. Relatives gave cash, generally half-a-crown, but there was little to spend it on.

The Home Guard, Women's Institute, Women's Guild and the Mothers' Union also laid on parties which were enjoyed, but none as lavish as the Navy's sponge trifles; maybe the musical chairs made up for it.

Several excellent theatrical shows including 'The Ghost Train' were produced by Tormentor officers and ratings to which villagers were invited and thoroughly enjoyed. Anne Shelton, the popular singer, also gave a performance to a packed theatre in 1944.

Most boys endeavoured to obtain regimental badges from soldiers with whom they or their families had become friends. These were proudly worn in their lapels or in a wide leather belt on the waist.

There were only two public houses in Warsash during the war, The Rising Sun and The Jolly Farmer at Fleet End. The Silver Fern, formerly Oakley's Café before the war, was used as a WVS canteen. The Salterns Working Men's Club, very much smaller then with a billiard table, in Newtown Road was a popular place. Most pubs did not serve meals; sometimes a pie may have been available.

King Neptune at the children's Christmas party at HMS Tormentor 1944

Members of the Salterns Working Mens Club, Boxing Day 1944

Planning for D-Day at Warsash began in 1943 with the conversion of Landing Craft Personnel vessels, which were required to undertake an extensive hydrographic survey of the Normandy coast.

The crews' tasks were to determine the gradient and type of surface on the beaches to plan for suitable routes into the beaches, with safe groundings for landing craft, tanks, vehicles and men. A survey was also conducted on the seabed, where the Mulberry harbours were to be positioned. These small LCPs were towed across the English Channel by motor gunboats, and made their own way for the final ten miles. The crews worked at night throughout the winter of 1943 to 1944, and often within a very short distance from the Germans. Leading Seaman Lewis Bryden, a coxswain in one of these vessels, was mentioned in despatches. He also received the DSM for his services during operations in Holland and married Warsash Wren Stella Packman in 1945. Fred Hartley also served in these vessels on D-Day as a flotilla shipwright. He married a Warsash girl and settled in Warsash after the war.

In March 1943 a new type of landing craft appeared on the river. This was the LCI, Landing Craft Infantry, similar in appearance to a motor torpedo boat, made of wood but of lighter construction. It could carry 100 troops at a speed of fifteen knots. Their crews were based in HMS Tormentor.

By November 1943 thirty LCIs had arrived with six to follow, and were moored upstream from the Ferry. Between May 1943 and the spring of 1944 the LCIs did intensive training with the commandos in a series of exercises. Heavy weather beaching trials were also carried out.

In early May the commandos were landed near Littlehampton, in terrain similar to that which would be found in their actual D-Day landings. Crossing the River Arun was similar to the Caen Canal and the Orne River in Normandy.

A small craft base named HMS Cricket was set up on the upper reaches of the Hamble River at Bursledon, where many commandos were trained.

The depot for anti-aircraft barrage balloons had been established earlier at Titchfield, in the buildings that later became the Plessey factory.

Large Canadian army camps in tents were erected and hidden in the trees at Fairthorne Manor at Curdridge. There were also British army camps at Sarisbury, Hamble and Netley. An American army camp was under canvas in Hook Park, and an American army medical unit operated in the buildings at Coldeast at Sarisbury. The very large army hospital at Netley was manned by American medical staff. It had a long pier running out into Southampton Water where ships could discharge patients who had been injured abroad.

The corridors in the hospital were so long that the Americans drove their jeeps along them. An American boat repair base was constructed on the foreshore at Hamble, with hundreds of lorry-loads of brick rubble brought from buildings which had been destroyed by bombing in Southampton.

Road blocks with sentries and checkpoints were in operation at the junction of Brook Lane and Barnes Lane, and at the crossroads in Warsash Road at Fleet End. Villagers could leave and return by showing their identity cards, but no other persons could enter without a special reason and supporting documents.

The Wrens were given a lecture on the importance of security. It was stressed that they were not to give the location of HMS Tormentor to anybody. A few days later a local Wren was at the Clock Tower crossroads when a large staff car flying a high ranking officer's flag stopped. The driver asked her the way to HMS Tormentor. Acting under orders she replied, "I do not know." He replied, "A Wren in uniform, in Warsash, and you do not know?" As it was a staff car she reluctantly gave the directions, thinking of the disciplinary procedures that may lay ahead if the driver had been undertaking a security check. It all seems humorous now, but it was a very serious situation at the time.

There were literally hundreds of craft in the river of many varied types and sizes. More anti-aircraft gun batteries and searchlight units were placed in the village to protect the fleet and the vehicles yet to come. Landing craft crews and troops practised assault landings on the beach on the Hook shoreline. As D-Day neared thousands of tanks, Bren gun carriers, field guns, anti-aircraft guns, lorries, ambulances, jeeps and motor cycles arrived, filling every road and spare piece of land, all parking nose to tail with their crews camping alongside for several weeks.

An anti-aircraft gun battery, surrounded by sandbags, was stationed in the field alongside Grooms, off Newtown Road. The gunners were annoyed because they thought their officers had been premature on 4th June in telling them to dismantle one of their tents. The tent was used for recreational purposes, writing letters etc, and yet they were still here on the evening of the 5th. The reason, unknown to the troops of course, was that General Eisenhower had postponed D-Day by twenty-four hours, waiting for the weather to improve. The gunners would often let children sit on the gun and turn the wheels that would train and elevate the gun barrel. The road past Grooms was never closed during the war, and there was access to the beach.

The Warsash-based LCPs were not used for landing assault troops after Dieppe; being built of plywood they could not withstand machine gun fire. Armour plate was fitted, but this reduced their speed. Nevertheless thirty-six of these craft were converted for smoke laying. Chlorosulphuric acid was pumped under pressure through a jet in the stern. As soon as the droplets of acid hit the air a huge cloud of white smoke was formed.

Lt Colin Kitching RNVR, the First Lieutenant of one of the three flotillas of LCPs, relates his memories prior to D-Day. "We left Warsash during the morning of 5th June 1944 to rendezvous with a fleet of ships at Calshot. The mood of the officers and ratings was remarkable, high-spirited bordering on ebullience. On previous operations their mood had been determined, but quiet and low key. The difference was that this was the day we had been waiting for, training for, and we knew that if things went well it was the beginning of the end of the long war in Europe.

"The journey eastward along The Solent was almost like a carnival. As one of the first assault groups to get on the move we passed scores of big ships of every kind, waiting their turn to sail.

"Soldiers crowded the rails of their troop transports and gave us, in our tiny craft, volleys of cheers. All these years later I am still touched when I think of it."

Of the 6,000 vessels to take part in the operation, the LCPs were the smallest to cross the Channel under their own power, and endured a force five wind at a speed of six knots, set by the slow-moving tank landing craft.

The smoke-laying LCPs were to be employed in the assault to cover bombarding warships, and to shield the DD swimming tanks after they had been launched from their carrying landing craft. However, the sea was very rough, and on Gold and Juno beaches the LCTs ran into the beach before discharging the tanks. The LCPs provided smoke screen cover for bombardment, and supply vessels during the following five weeks.

During the afternoon of 5th June 1944 as children cycled to school, lorries carrying the 1st Special Service Commando Brigade, including two troops of French commandos, passed on their way to Warsash. A total of 3,000 men embarked into the thirty-six Warsash LCIs at The Rising Sun jetties.

In the leading craft were Brigadier the Lord Lovat DSO, MC and Scots piper Bill Millin, who played his bagpipes on the landing craft as they left Warsash, and on the beach in Normandy.

Most of the small craft that survived the assault were based on the French coast for three months undertaking ferrying and certain mine-sweeping duties.

Once the fleet had sailed boys and girls spent much time on the foreshore,

Brigadier Lord Lovat's piper plays on Strawberry Field at Warsash before embarking on landing craft on 5th June 1944. Photograph courtesy of the Imperial War Museum, London, negative number H39039

Commandos with their bicycles boarding landing craft near The Rising Sun Hotel 5th June 1944. Photograph courtesy of the Imperial War Museum, London, negative number H39046

Commandos embarked in the Warsash-based landing craft, en-route for Normandy on 5th June 1944.
Photograph courtesy of the Imperial War Museum, London, negative number H39041

collecting American army 24-hour food packs that floated in containing Nescafé which we had never heard of, let alone seen before, chocolate, strips of chewing gum, a prize indeed, and tins of emergency ration ships' biscuits. There were crates of oranges that we had not seen during the war, but these were always waterlogged and inedible.

After several days in Normandy some of the Warsash crews and craft returned to the Hamble River carrying wounded servicemen, French civilians and German prisoners of war. Many of the craft had been damaged and needed repairs, others were wrecked and laying on French beaches.

The Salterns medical centre was used as a casualty clearing station prior to transporting patients to hospitals in Haslar, Southampton and Portsmouth.

The Warsash LCPs were employed later at Walcheren in Holland in October 1944 to survey the beaches, and to lay down a protective smoke shield. They guided the assault craft to the beach and were involved in a very fierce action.

During the operations eight craft were lost in Normandy and one in Walcheren, although many others were severely damaged.

For its work in Normandy the LCI and LCP squadrons were awarded six DSCs, three DSMs and seventeen Mentioned in Despatches (four posthumously). There was one DSM and several Mentioned in Despatches in Walcheren.

In early 1945 the 702 LCP flotilla was carried across Europe on army tank-transporting vehicles. The vessels were launched into the Rhine River to assist the Royal Engineers who were building pontoon bridges, and to make smoke if required to veil the engineers from aircraft attack or shelling.

Soon after D-Day one of the first German flying bombs (VI) known as Doodlebugs landed in the rhododendron woods near St Mary's Church, blowing out all the stained-glass windows. Leaves were scattered as far as Newtown Road in one direction and Locks Heath in the other. Everyone in Warsash heard the noise of the aircraft, and knew that when the engine stopped it was coming down, and that you may well be the target. There had been no air raid alert, so people lay flat wherever they were, or dived for cover in the cupboard under the stairs.

Although life for service personnel and civilians was tense and worrying, there were on occasions humorous situations, as in the text that follows relating to a visit to HMS Tormentor by the Medical Director General of the Royal Navy, described by Surgeon Lt Michael Holloway RNVR.

"Some five weeks or so after D-Day we received a signal from Surgeon Vice Admiral Sir Sheldon Dudley that he wished to pay an informal visit to Tormentor to see how things were being done, and to enquire as to how we were dealing with casualties from the 'other side'.

"As the pressure was now off, and we had sailed virtually all our LCPs and LCIs, it was felt that we could put on something of a show for the old boy.

"On the appointed day he arrived by car, flying a Vice Admiral's flag and accompanied by his deputy, Surgeon Rear Admiral Griffith. They were piped aboard, which was Captain Billy Byles's idea, and visited our sick bay in The Salterns (now Admirals House) which they much admired, especially Sheila Neary, our prettiest VAD (nurse) who brought in their coffee.

"After a slap-up lunch with Uncle Bill, (the captain) we took them down to the yard where they embarked on an LCP crewed by the shapeliest boat crew that could be found. They had a short cruise as far as the Mercury training ship, and then back to The Salterns for tea. This was quite an eye-opener for them as Sister Downey produced the biggest bowl of raspberries that I have ever seen; soft fruit had not been seen in London for about three years. At the end of the repast Admiral Griffith remarked wistfully that he wouldn't mind taking the remainder home with him if a box could be found. However, the MDG remarked tartly, 'Don't be ridiculous, Charlie, you'd only sit on them, and get them all over your trousers.' So he did not get them, but he had the last crack, saying to me as they were departing, 'I don't know how you managed to wangle this appointment, but I can assure you that if I'd had any idea what it was like here, I would have taken it for myself, and you would have not come near it.'"

Relationships between the services and the civilian villagers were always very good. Service personnel were welcome in The Salterns Club. They were officially not allowed to wear civilian clothes ashore, but Wrens would call at a friendly house and change into a civilian dress to spend an evening with a boyfriend. Several young people living in London, who were relatives of service personnel, came and stayed in the village for a period while London was being attacked by the German V2 rocket bombs in 1944.

As the European war came to an end there were celebrations. A huge bonfire was built from driftwood in the gun emplacement at Hook Point by Royal Navy personnel. Two ratings were pouring petrol from large cans onto the wood when someone threw in a lighted match. There was a violent explosion, knocking everyone down; some went over the sea wall, which at that time was five feet high. The unfortunate ratings suffered extremely severe burns to their faces and hands, and had a long walk for treatment at the Tormentor sick bay.

On VE night, 8th May 1945, a huge bonfire was built at the crossroads by the Clock Tower. The pillbox had been demolished by then, and anything that would burn was placed on the fire, including dinghies that were carried from the shore. Mrs McCall's piano was brought out of the front room of her cottage in Shore Road, and the party went on all night.

HMS Tormentor was run down and closed in May 1946. A plinth was erected on the War Memorial at the Victory Hall engraved with the names of the sixteen Warsash men who died in the armed services during the war.

Many of the RN vessels at Warsash were sold and converted to yachts or houseboats; several of these were berthed at Swanwick shore near the famous J Class yachts Endeavour and Velsheda that were being used as houseboats.

HMS Tormentor's base in Newtown Road became the School of Navigation for young Merchant Navy officer cadets,

A German yacht, seized as wartime reparations, which broke away from her moorings at Calshot during a storm in 1945 and became beached at Hook, with the author's wife swinging in the rigging being pushed by her cousin Dawn

who marched to church in uniform on Sundays. The Rising Sun jetties were removed, and strawberries resumed their place of prominence and were again sent by road and rail all over the country.

Yachts appeared on the river, and the boat yards were concentrating on private work. Virtually everyone who used the river was able to scull a dinghy, that is propelling it with one oar over the stern, but the village where everyone knew everyone had gone for ever.

Since the Second World War the men and women who served at HMS Tormentor as staff, landing craft crews or commandos have held reunions in The Rising Sun, which have been well attended. On Sunday 6th June 2004, the 60th anniversary of D-Day, a Remembrance Service was held in the car park opposite The Rising Sun conducted by the Reverend Andrew Norris, with the Warsash Brass Band in attendance. Paying their respects were fifty ex-service veterans. The Commodore of HMS Collingwood and the Mayor of Fareham laid wreaths on the D-Day memorial, which is designed to represent the bow and raised ramp of a landing craft. Several hundred people gathered to witness this memorable day.

After taking lunch in The Rising Sun or Shore House, the veterans came to the Victory Hall for tea, where the D-Day photos from local collections were displayed. Many of the veterans and their relatives had travelled from all over Britain, including the Shetland Islands. Several people were looking for information regarding their fathers' and grandfathers' exploits, and of the landing craft that took them to France.

A street party outside The Jolly Farmer Public House in Fleet End to celebrate the end of the Second World War. The writing on the wall 'Fielders Ales' relates to the owners of the premises, who also ran a brewery in Titchfield

Street party at The Jolly Farmer to celebrate the victory over Japan and the end of the Second World War

Surgeries, shops and services in Warsash during the years 1940 to 1950

Doctor Dr Kingdon held a surgery in his house in Locks Road, Locks Heath, treating the Warsash villagers. He was joined by his son John, who entered the army during the Second World War, returning to take over the practice in 1945. They were well respected, would diagnose patients in their surgery, and mix the medicine themselves.

Dr Mackie practised at Sarisbury, and Dr Shakespeare at Park Gate.

Midwife Most children were born at home, with the midwife, Nurse Hill, residing in Fleet End.

Dentist The school dentist held his surgery in the British Legion rooms at Park Gate.

Bank Martins Bank used a room in a private house in Shore Road to conduct business for a limited number of hours each week.

During this period there were at least twenty retail shops in Warsash, plus several other traders from outside the village.

Hardware Miss N Button ran a shop for Mr Edmunds in the Corner Garage.

Sweet Shop Mr Trow sold only cigarettes, chocolates and confectionery in his shop in Warsash Road, next to Oakley's café where The Silver Fern Inn now stands.

Haberdashers and Wool Mrs Harbinson owned a shop in Warsash Road, situated between Mr Trow's and the Victory Hall.

Mrs Olden ran a shop located in her house at Fleet End Corner.

Post Office Mrs Sullivan and her daughter Eileen ran the office on the north side of Warsash Road at the Dibles Road junction, with telegrams also being delivered from this office.

There was also a small office in Heath Road, Locks Heath, used by Warsash residents.

One postman only delivered all the mail for Fleet End and Warsash.

Bicycle and Radio Repairs Edmunds Garage in Warsash Road.

Police The Police house was in the adjoining property to the Post Office.

Newsagent Mrs Poulton kept a shop next to the Police house until 1950, when the business was taken over by Mr Roy Knight.

Shoe Repairs Mr Read worked in a small workshop in the rear garden of the newsagents.

Butchers Mr Palmer at the junction of Warsash and Dibles Roads.

Mr Collins in Shore Road.

Baker St John's shop in Dibles Road with their bakery in Titchfield.

Chemist Everett the chemist, next to the baker's in Dibles Road, with a pharmacy for prescriptions at Park Gate.

Coal Merchant Mr C Sandy with his yard in Osborne Road, with his assistant Mr R Buckett.

Fish and Chips Mr Marshall's shop was opposite the Post Office in Warsash Road.

Petrol and Vehicle Repairs Edmunds Garage, Warsash Corner.

Collins Garage, Warsash Corner.

Grocers Mr Hayes in Warsash Road, Fleet End, a few yards from the school.

Mr Fox at Warsash Corner.

Mr Waters in Newtown Road.

There was a number of small shops that sold a smaller choice of grocer's items.

Mrs Jones in Osborne Road and Mrs Searle in Osborne Road.

Mr Crudgington in Fleet End Road and Mrs Green at Greens Corner, Fleet End.

Mrs Winter in Warsash Road, Fleet End.

Mrs Edmondson in Brook Lane, Sarisbury, was frequented by Warsash residents.

Gents Hairdresser Mr Olden at Fleet End Corner, Mr S Knapp in Warsash Road.

Ladies Hairdresser Mrs Blackwell opened a shop in Shore Road in the coach house.

Taxi Mr Alan Edwards operated a service also from the old coach house.

Mr Edmunds operated a service from Edmunds Garage.

Fresh Fish Mr George Arnold supplied fish from his shop, also situated in the former coach house.

Library A private lending library was situated also in the coach house room at Clock Tower Buildings.

Yacht Broker Mr Bradshaw was in business, also in a part of the coach house.

Antique Shop Good quality items were sold in a 19th century cottage shop near The Rising Sun.

Insurance Mr Rowe, who resided in Church Road, represented the Prudential Assurance Company.

Boatbuilder and Joiner Geoff Rowe built small dinghies and undertook joinery work in his workshop behind the Clock Tower.

Furniture Sales Jack Boardman sold second-hand furniture in the ex-Home Guard drill hall in Warsash Road.

House Builder Mr Wyn Newbury with his office and workshop in Warsash Road.

Painter and Decorator Mr F Edwards with his house and workshop next to Oakley's Café.

Cafés Mrs Fuger's in Shore Road and Oakley's in Warsash Road.

Public Houses The Rising Sun in Warsash and The Jolly Farmer in Fleet End.

Hotels, Clubs and Restaurants The Hamblemeads Hotel in Newtown Road.

The Salterns Working Men's Club in Newtown Road.

Buses The Southdown and Hants and Dorset bus companies ran services every half-hour to Fareham and Portsmouth, and to Southampton hourly.

Hauliers and Carriers Bert Green with his lorry in Osborne Road.

Clem Boyes with his large van in Warsash Road.

Mr Peckham with his lorry in Greenaways Lane.

Undertaker Mr Septimus Newbury, who resided in the house now The Ferryman.

Traders from outside the village also made deliveries to Warsash homes; these were:

Carrier Mr Cleeves delivered packages in his van, which had been carried by rail to the local stations.

Milk Oakley's from their farm at Curdridge.

Yates and Hounsome from Park Gate.

In the early 1940s milk was delivered by pail, and ladled into the housewives' jugs.

Bread Newbury from their Sarisbury bakery.

Meat Mr C Humby from his butcher's shop at Park Gate.

Paraffin (used for heating) Oily Williams from Titchfield; he also sold saucepans and household items, a proverbial market on wheels.

Knitting needles, pins, ribbons, tapes A Sikh would be welcomed on his annual visit, carrying a large suitcase. He visited homes with high quality goods that were essential requirements for housewives, and not available anywhere else in the district.

Fred Dyke's steam lorry at Fleet End crossroads, carrying gravel from the extraction pits in Warsash
Courtesy of Mr Frank Claxton

Well-known persons who have resided in Hook Park and Warsash

William Hornby Esquire, former Governor of Bombay, of Hook House

Captain Foote RN of Passage House

Admiral Lord Thomas Cochrane RN of Passage House

Captain Archibald Swinton RN of Passage House

Mr James Lock, entrepreneur, fishing fleet, restaurant and property owner

Mr Edward Sartoris, MP of Passage House, renamed Warsash House

Mrs Adelaide Sartoris née Kemble, opera singer

Mr Algernon Sartoris of Warsash House

Mrs Nellie Sartoris, daughter of President Grant of the USA

Admiral Wemyss, First Lord of the Admiralty of Warsash Lodge

Mr George Shenley of Warsash House

Sir Warden Chilcott, MP of The Salterns, land speculator, yachtsman

Mr Walter Greenhill of Hamble Bank, England and Sussex cricketer

Sir Maurice Jenks, former Lord Mayor of London, of Sunburst in Hook

Contessa Rosamond di Sant'Elia, owner of Springfields, now named Kingswood House, in Newtown Road

Sir Austen Chamberlain, British Foreign Secretary, of Hamblemeads, Newtown Road

Montague Grahame-White, early motorist and owner of many steam yachts, of Warsash House

Lord Stalbridge of Warsash House, race horse owner and Fastnet Race winner in 1927

Sir Ralph Richardson, actor, of Red Tiles in Newtown Road

Sir Laurence Olivier, actor, of Hook Park

Vivienne Leigh, actress, of Hook Park

Lt Phillipe de Gaulle, Free French Navy, son of General de Gaulle, in HMS Tormentor

Wren Patricia Mountbatten, in HMS Tormentor, later to be Countess Mountbatten, daughter of Lord Louis Mountbatten

Cdr Douglas Fairbanks Jnr, USNR, in HMS Tormentor

Sir Alec Rose in HMS Tormentor

Mrs Ruth Ellis, the last woman to be hanged in England, of Warsash Road

Rear Admiral Scatchard DSC and two bars of Newtown Road

Lord Ellenborough of Warsash Lodge

Mr Peter Twiss OBE DSC of Brook Lane

Miss Ethel Gee, born and resided in Warsash, jailed for espionage at Portland for the Russians

Well-known persons who have visited Warsash, Hook and Chilling

George Parsons, who constructed wooden warships in Warsash

President Ulysses Grant of the USA, formerly General Grant, visited Warsash House with his wife Julia

King George VII visited Warsash House when he was Prince of Wales

Lord Louis Mountbatten visited HMS Tormentor

Miss Anne Shelton, singer, who gave a perfomance at HMS Tormentor

Lord Lovat, en route to Normandy in 1944

HRH Prince Philip at HMS Tormentor

HRH Prince Charles visited the Royal Thames Yacht Club in 1975

HRH Princess Margaret by helicopter, en route for Swanwick

Lord Birkenhead, Lord Chancellor and yacht owner

Winston Churchill visiting Sir Warden Chilcott

Mr Claude Grahame-White, early aviator, visited Warsash House

Dame Clara Butt, famous contralto noted for Land of Hope and Glory, sang in the Victory Hall

Mr Kennerley Rumfold, singer

Sir Thomas Sopwith, aircraft manufacturer and J Class yacht owner

Mr Harry Hawker, aircraft manufacturer

Lord Tollemache, early motorist

Mrs Assheton Harbord, pioneer balloonist

Miss Gertrude Lawrence, actress visiting Chilling House

Lt Col David Niven, actor, visiting Chilling House

HRH The Princess Royal for the opening ceremony of Warsash Sailing Club's building development in 1994

Bibliography

With thanks for permission to use extracts and images from the following books:

Course, Dr C, *The Southampton and Netley Railway*, published by Southampton City Council

Baker-White, J, *True Blue*, Frederick Muller, reprinted by permission of the Random House Group Ltd

Liddle, P, *D-Day: By Those Who Were There*, Pen and Sword Books. A short extract has been taken from the book, regarding the experiences of Lt Colin Kitching RNVR, Retired

Scott, K, *HMS Tormentor, 1940-1946 A Brief History*

Twiss, P, *Faster than the Sun*, Grub Street Publishing Ltd

A drawing by artist Ray Woodward has been used from *The Wooden Fighting Ship of the Royal Navy* by E E H Archibald, Blandford Press, also a small amount of text and several images from *At the Wheel, Ashore and Afloat*, G T Foulis and Co, 1935. Attempts to contact the rights owners have been unsuccessful, therefore would they please contact Warsash Publishing.

Acknowledgements

Thanks are given to the following organisations and persons, for providing information, photographs or illustrations.

British Aircraft Directory

Mr Matt Durrant

Library of Congress, Washington DC
USA Handy Collection

Richard, Austin and Wyatt Estate Agents

Chatham Historic Dockyard Trust, with images of HMS Gannet, where the ship is open to the public
idoulton@chdt.org.uk

Imperial War Museum

Thomas Ross Collection
www.rosscollection.co.uk

Crown Copyright and Landmark Information Group Ltd (all rights reserved 2006)

Kimbell Art Museum, Fort Worth Texas

Military Heraldry Society

Minelayers and Sweepers,
Mr Rik Furnival

News Portsmouth

Southern Daily Echo

Through Mighty Ships website
Mr Tim Latham

TS Mercury Association
Mr Richard Briggs

Times Literary Supplement

Topham Picturepoint

Warsash Maritime Academy
Mr John Millican and
Mrs Therese Barker

Levens Hall, Kendal, Cumbria
Mr C H Bagot

United Kingdom Fortifications Club

Mrs Barbara Bolt, Queensland, Australia

Mr Frank Bowman

Mr Rob Burnage

Mr Roy Childs

Mr Frank Claxton

Mrs Jocelyn Clyne

Mrs Joan Collins

Mr Philly Coombs

Mr Bryan Cozens

Mr Frank Claxton

Mr Paul Eustace

Mr Bert Foy

Mrs Betty Fuller

Mr George Fuller

Mr Charles Fuger

Mr John Hampton

Mrs Miriam Hampton

Mr Trevor Harvey

Mr and Mrs Chris Horsler

Mr Roy Knight

Lt Colin Kitching RNVR Retired

Mrs Heather Maynard

Mr Graham Moody

Mr and Mrs Simon Nash

Mr Harry Pannell

Mrs Ellen Peters

Mr John Rowe

Mr Peter Sandbach

Mr A H Swinton

Mr Keith Taylor

Miss Jane Thakker

Mr and Mrs Duncan Williams

Mrs Mona Willis

Index, with illustrations in **bold**, and coloured prints denoted with the prefix **Col**

Index

Index

The schooner Tom Roper which carried pig iron from the blast furnace in Warsash to Honfleur and Paris

The sailing cutter Tally Ho, with a Warsash owner and skipper, won the third Fastnet race in 1927

A model replica of HMS Hotspur is displayed in a prominent position in St Mary's Church, Warsash, whilst a similar model rests in a glass case in Levens Hall, Cumbria, which is open to the public (Author)

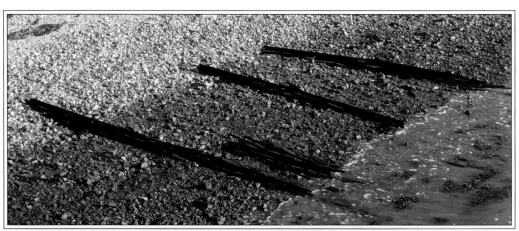

The wooden launchways, which were used to launch the warships built in Warsash between 1807 and 1813. They can be seen laying in the beach in their original position, three metres south of the Warsash Sailing Club jetty (Author)

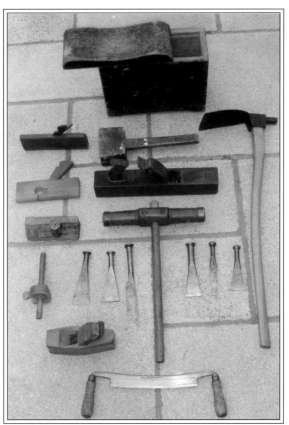

A small part of a shipwright's tool kit which includes a draw knife, an adze, a caulking mallet, with caulking irons and a box seat. A number of wooden planes are also shown, one with a round sole (Author)

Blazer badge worn by Royal Naval Shipwright Artificers (Author)

The first TS Mercury, ex-sailing barque Illova, moored off Binstead in the Isle of Wight in 1890.
The vessel moved to moorings in the Hamble River in 1892, remaining until 1916

The second TS Mercury, which moored in the Hamble River from 1914 to 1980, formerly HMS Gannet

Chatham Historic Dockyard Trust has restored TS Mercury/HMS Gannet to her original 1878 condition, where she is open to the public

The restored figurehead of TS Mercury/HMS Gannet

The dairy of the Warsash House Estate, built in Brook Lane in 1914, with a modern dwelling skilfully attached (Author)

The Rising Sun public house built in 1906 overlooks the river at Warsash (Author)

Tumbleweeds, in Shore Road, formerly two Warsash House Estate cottages built circa 1800

Willow Tree Cottage in Dibles Road built circa 1750

The Salterns, Sir Warden Chilcott's residence in Newtown Road, now known as Admirals House (Author)

Sir Warden Chilcott's brigantine Dolphin

Golf House, in Hook Park, built as the coach house for Hook House circa 1790 (Author)

Hook Cottages in Hook Village, built as homes for the Hornby Estate workers, circa 1849 (Author)

Fish House in Chilling Lane built circa 1850 (Author)

Margaret Woodford, the author's wife, in conversation with Rt Hon the Countess Patricia Mountbatten of Burma, who opened the new library at the College of Maritime Studies, now Warsash Maritime Academy, in 1989. The Countess served at Warsash as a Wren in the Royal Navy during the Second World War

The Warsash Maritime Academy and the Hamble River in 2006

This plinth, in the foreshore at Warsash, commemorates the British and Allied commando units who sailed from the Hamble River on 5th June 1944 for the D-Day landings in Normandy (Author)

The memorial to the men of Warsash who did not return after the First and Second World Wars (Author)